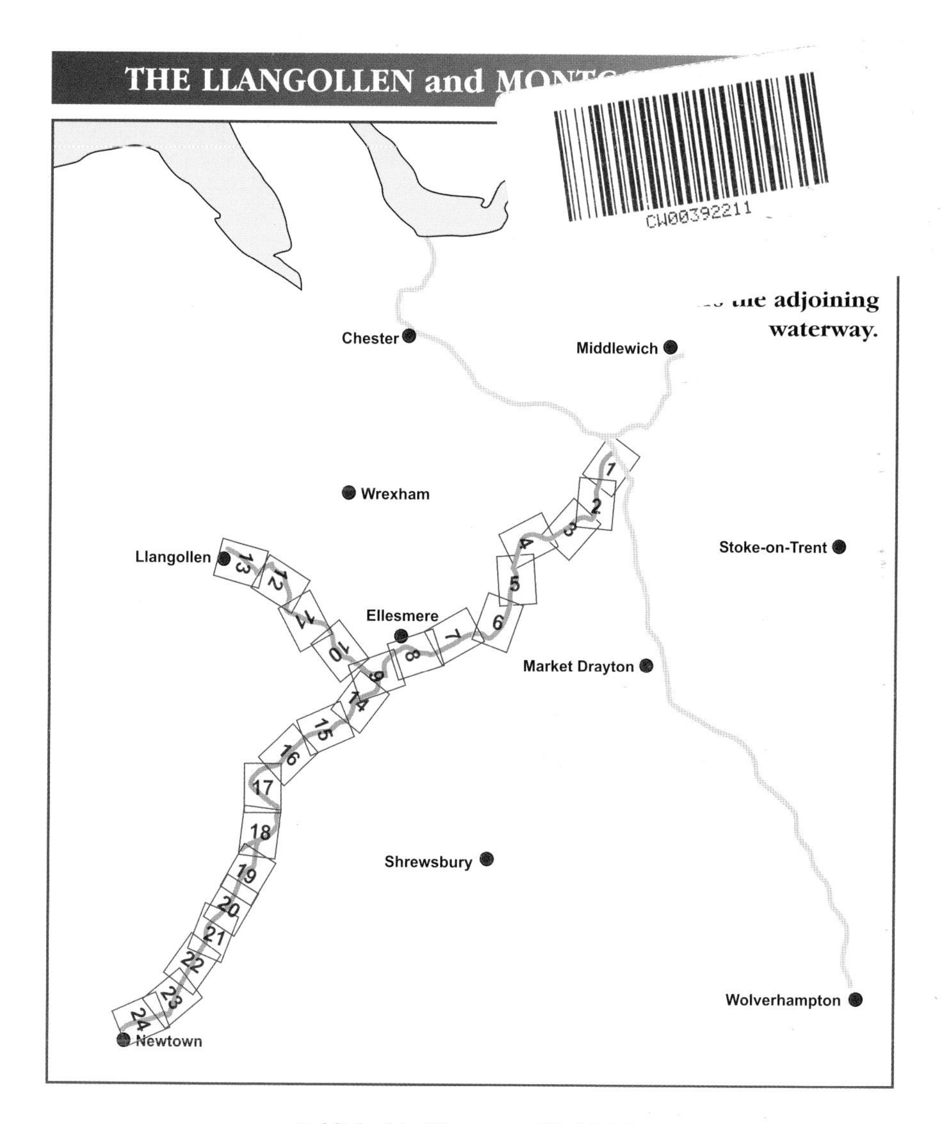

Published by Waterways World Ltd,
151 Station Street, Burton-on-Trent, Staffordshire DE14 IBG, England
Revised and Edited by Euan Corrie
Original Research by Hugh Potter and David Harris
Maps by Branch Out Design, Bretby, Burton-on-Trent

Seventh Edition 2005

One of a series of guides covering the Inland Waterways of England and Wales

British Library Cataloguing in Publication Data
A catalogue record for this book is available from the British Library
ISBN 1 870002 89 X
Printed in the United Kingdom by Information Press, Oxford

INTRODUCTION

This Guide covers in detail the Llangollen Canal between Hurleston Junction on the Shropshire Union Canal's Main Line, near Nantwich in Cheshire, and Llantisilio where it draws its water supply from the river Dee above Llangollen. Historically, the Llangollen was a part of the Shropshire Union system along with the Montgomery Canal, which is also covered from its junction with the Llangollen at Welsh Frankton to Newtown. Restoration work continues apace opening more of the Montgomery to navigation and full details of currently navigable waters and walking routes along the unnavigable sections are given in these pages.

This new edition has been thoroughly revised and everything that the first-time boat hirer or the already experienced navigator needs to know about the route that lies before him is included. It contains information about navigating the waterway, facilities for boating and shopping, and places of interest within walking distance of the canal. Moreover, towpath walkers and those who enjoy exploring canals by car are also catered for. So, whatever your interests are, we hope that you will find this guide useful. Have a good trip, remember the Country Code and enjoy discovering the Llangollen and Montgomery canals.

Acknowledgements

The editor is grateful to a great many people who have assisted in the production of this guide. In particular Hugh Potter and David Harris who undertook the research for previous editions; Philippa Corrie acted as boat captain, car navigator, clerk and secretary on subsequent trips. Thanks are also due to The Quinta Christian Centre near Chirk (www.quinta.org), especially Peter; to Adam at Alvechurch Boat Centre's base at Wrenbury for boatyard services well beyond the call of normal duty and to Duncan Pottinger who wielded the cutting gear; to Tony and Mary Lewery and to the staff of British Waterways. The Aylesbury Canal Society's Launderette List is, as always, an invaluable aid.

The Llangollen and Montgomery canals – A Brief History

The history of the Llangollen and Montgomery canals (as they are now called) is complex and those interested in researching it in detail are referred to the works of Hadfield and Wilson (see Bibliography on page 12).

The original plan, proposed by a group of industrialists from around Ellesmere and Ruabon, for a canal linking the Mersey, at what is now Ellesmere Port, with the Severn at Shrewsbury via Ellesmere was never achieved. The Act was passed in 1793 but the canal, engineered by William Jessop and later by Thomas Telford, that finally opened in 1805 was very different from the one originally proposed. It was largely the canal that we know today from the north side of Pontcysyllte Aqueduct through Chirk, Welsh Frankton, Ellesmere and Wrenbury to Hurleston, near Nantwich, where it joined the Chester Canal (now the Shropshire Union Canal Main Line).

The Montgomery Canal was built as three separate canals: a northern section from the junction with the Llangollen at Welsh Frankton to Llanymynech (originally a branch of the Ellesmere – now renamed Llangollen – Canal), opened in 1796; an eastern section from Llanymynech to Garthmyl, opened in 1797; and a western branch from Garthmyl to Newtown opened in 1819. Its total length was 35 miles.

Other branches led to Edstaston (part way to Prees) and there were short arms to Ellesmere and to Whitchurch. The line from north of Pontcysyllte to Llantisilio – generally considered the most attractive part of the canal today – was opened in 1808 as a navigable water feeder. Of the remainder of the proposed line continuing northwards from Pontcysyllte, which was to include a 4,608-yard tunnel, the only significant section to be built was the 'Wirral Line' between Chester and Ellesmere Port (being the first part to be opened, in 1795) and still in use today as part of the Shropshire Union Canal's Main Line. The name of Ellesmere Port (formerly Netherpool) originated from the proposed line of canal that was never directly completed – it was to be the port for the Shropshire town of Ellesmere. The locals' and working boaters' habit of referring to this town as 'The Port' originated from the need to distinguish it from its Shropshire parent.

There were several amalgamations and name changes to the canals over the years, the most significant probably being the amalgamation into the Shropshire Union Railways & Canal Co in 1845–46.

Through traffic ceased on the section below Frankton Locks in 1936 following a breach between the Perry Aqueduct and Frankton Locks.

Commercial traffic had ceased elsewhere by the end of the 1930s and in 1944 – a fateful year for Britain's waterways – the entire system based on the original Ellesmere Canal was abandoned by Act of Parliament promoted by the canal's owners, the London Midland & Scottish Railway. The section we know now as the Llangollen Canal was retained for use as a water supply channel. The Montgomery Canal section was temporarily repaired, to allow boats trapped below the breach to escape, before the canal was allowed to subside into dereliction. The Abandonment Act allowed highway authorities to demolish hump-backed road bridges and realign carriageways across the canal creating water-level obstructions to navigation.

Maintenance of the water supply channel was to be the salvation of the Llangollen to Hurleston route; pleasure cruising as we know it today was almost unheard of in 1944, although this was the year in which the late L.T.C. Rolt's famous book *Narrow Boat* was published. As a result of *Narrow Boat*, and the formation of the Inland Waterways Association in 1946, the possibilities of pleasure cruising on the canals began to be realised and several companies started hiring boats. Many of these were in the North-West of England and the early hirers almost always headed for the Llangollen Canal.

In 1967, the Shropshire Union Canal Society began a feasibility study of the Montgomery Canal's restoration possibilities. In the same year that their report came out, 1968, plans were advanced to build a bypass for Welshpool along the course of the canal through the centre of the town, as a section of the proposed Liverpool–Swansea trunk road. This had the effect of uniting local and national opposition to the road scheme, and, following a 'big dig' at Welshpool organised by the Shropshire Union Canal Society, the Waterway Recovery Group and the IWA, the restoration movement for the Montgomery Canal took off.

The attempt to re-open the Montgomery has already involved several bodies. These include the Prince of Wales' Committee, which administered the re-opening of the 'Seven Miles' section north of Welshpool; Shropshire

Union Canal Society; Inland Waterways Association; Waterway Recovery Group; local authorities; Welsh Development Agency and Wales Tourist Board. Co-ordinating the restoration project is the Montgomery Waterway Restoration Trust, which liaises between the various groups and British Waterways, who manage the canal.

Today, much of Britain's canal system is available for cruising and further lengths, as well as the Montgomery, are being restored, but there is no doubt that the Llangollen Canal is still the most popular.

In 1987 BW obtained an Act of Parliament to legally facilitate restoration of the Montgomery – the first such Act for the reopening of a waterway.

Navigating the Llangollen and Montgomery Canals

Don't forget, if you are thinking of an excursion to the Montgomery Canal that it is not navigable throughout, although at the time of writing it is accessible to craft leaving the Llangollen at Frankton as far as Gronwen Wharf and over several disconnected lengths further south. It may be advisable to check with British Waterways as to what progress has been made with extension and connecting up these lengths or what arrangements are needed to use slipways on the disconnected sections. Small craft using isolated sections of canal require a licence just as much as full sized narrowboats on the main waterway system.

Licences

Addresses of all the authorities and organisations that can provide further information are listed on page 12.

All craft, whether powered or unpowered, including canoes and dinghies, must have a British Waterways Boat Licence when navigating the Llangollen and Montgomery canals, or indeed, the rest of the connected canal system. Details of licensing are obtainable from the General Managers at Birmingham or Northwich or from British Waterways' Watford headquarters (see Useful Addresses on page 12).

Stoppages

From time to time, particularly in the winter months (November–March), it may become necessary for British Waterways to carry out maintenance work on the waterway. Alternatively, a dry spring or summer may result in restrictions due to shortage of water. Either of these circumstances may result in sections being closed or 'stopped'. Details of stoppages are published monthly in *Waterways World* magazine and are usually available on www.waterscape.com. For unscheduled stoppages telephone Canalphone North (01923 201401). To obtain assistance or report emergencies outside office hours dial 0800 4799947 for Freephone Canals. Have details of the waterway and the nearest lock or bridge number or similar landmark ready.

Water

The Llangollen Canal is well blessed with water supplies as a result of its function as a supply conduit to the Crewe and Nantwich area. However, some boaters will consider this blessing a mixed one when contemplating entering or leaving the locks across the strong flow around their by-wash channels. The Montgomery Canal is much less favoured, as supply towards Hurleston must take priority. However, both canals are shallow all along the edges except at old wharves and recognised tying up places. No matter what the prevailing weather conditions all the water you use in locks has to be supplied from the pounds upstream so use it wisely – CONSERVE IT! Share locks, if boat length allows, wait for oncoming boats if the lock is in their favour (even if it costs you five minutes, that's better than a dry pound!) and always ensure that all the gates and paddles are closed before leaving a lock unless an approaching boat obviously intends to use it. There is no point in rushing into a short pound in the lock flights that is already occupied by a boat going in your direction – the water you empty from the lock will simply run over the weir to waste. Remember – 'One Up, One Down' saves water and time in the long run.

Flow It will take you longer to get up to Llangollen than it will to get back. This is because of the flow of water – some 96 million gallons a week – which supplies the reservoir adjacent to Hurleston Junction from the Horseshoe Falls at Llantisilio. It is the supply of this water, a major source for mid-Cheshire, that saved the canal for navigation following the Abandonment Act of 1944. However, this flow down the canal, particularly through narrow, shallow sections like Chirk Tunnel, will make a considerable difference to the speed of your boat. The best thing to do is just to let the engine push you along on tickover and admire the wonderful scenery. Under no circumstances must you create a breaking wash; you may be reported to BW or your hire company for this and many companies retain the damage deposits of boats reported.

By-washes Another effect of the great flow down the canal is that the by-washes (the channels that take the water around the locks) run very strongly and these can affect your steering, especially when entering a lock from below. You will usually see this minor torrent of water flowing back into the main canal immediately below each lock and if you are steering straight for the lock it will almost certainly throw the bows of your boat across before you have time to correct your course. If you see the outflow, the best thing to do is to steer towards it, anticipating its effect.

One-way traffic Towards Llangollen there are certain lengths of canal that are too narrow for boats to pass each other. A little common sense here should save a head-on confrontation.

Speed

There is a speed limit of 4mph on the canal. Even this low speed is often too fast. Remember – an excessive wash or breaking wave causes bank erosion and damage to moored craft as well as being a general nuisance. If the wash from the stern starts to break up the banks EASE OFF, and you'll probably find that your speed in relation to terra-firma will increase anyway. Be particularly watchful of your wash on the Montgomery where there are important flora and fauna, which developed along the canal during its derelict period. Slow down when approaching or passing moored craft, other craft under way, locks, bridges, tunnels, engineering works and on bends. When the view ahead is obstructed, slow down, sound your horn and listen.

Rule of the Road

Craft meeting should steer to the right and pass each other left to left. If you do not intend to do this you must make it clear to the oncoming boat. When a vessel is being towed from the bank pass outside the vessel to avoid fouling the towing line – never pass between the towed vessel and the bank. Craft travelling with the current on rivers or tideway have the right of way over those heading against the flow.

Depth

If you could see the canal drained of its water you'd be surprised how shallow it is, especially at the edges, the cross section being a shallow 'V' rather than 'U' shaped. Keep to the centre of the channel except when passing oncoming boats. Give way to larger craft, which require deeper water. You may find yourself aground if you have moved out of the centre channel to pass another boat. This is nothing to worry about. You should be able to reverse off, but if that doesn't work, push yourself off with your boat pole.

The lockside at Hurleston used to be adorned with a British Waterways' notice warning of severe restriction of draft further up the canal but matters are much improved these days. Much of the research for this guide was undertaken in a former Grand Union Canal Carrying Co working boat but this vessel is navigated with care by somebody who has been at the same tiller for over 25 years. Modern pleasure craft should experience no difficulty in reaching Llangollen Wharf.

Draft is now no problem along this canal given skillful steering and resolve not to try and tie up away from recognised moorings. The earliest concrete-lined section of the feeder between Trevor and Llangollen and that by the Sun Trevor Hotel will only cause difficulty at more than about 2ft 6in draft before the channel has been scoured out by spring boat traffic. The approach to Llangollen Wharf is also slow but there is no problem in turning once you have arrived.

Mooring

Always, unless specifically indicated to the contrary, moor against the towpath side of the canal. Steer your boat in bow first, put the engine into neutral and then pull the stern of your boat in with your rope. Keeping the propeller turning near to the bank could seriously damage the propeller and both the bed and bank of the canal. When pushing off again, ensure that the boat is well away from the bank before engaging forward gear.

Try to avoid using mooring spikes on the high embankments where any leaks they might encourage could be disastrous – mooring is prohibited in some places for this reason.

- *Do not* moor too near bridges or locks so as to obstruct full size craft cruising the canal.
- *Do not* moor on bends or in winding holes.
- *Do not* moor in the short pounds of a flight of locks.
- *Do not* stretch ropes across towpaths where they will obstruct and endanger towpath users.
- *Never* run your engine in gear when the boat is tied up, this rapidly erodes the bank and undermines even quite deep piling, not to mention creating a pile of silt in the middle of the channel a few yards astern. Apart from that it's against the canal bye-laws!

Safety First

Remember always that prevention is better than cure. Wear non-slip footwear and beware of slippery lock sides and gates in wet weather. Beware of low bridges – some of which are lower in the middle (sometimes with supporting girders) than at each end. Make sure that your crew – especially those sitting on the cabin top – is aware of the presence of a low bridge. Before you enter a long tunnel, tell the crew to switch on the cabin lights (the cabin lights shining on the walls are useful to the helmsman). Ensure that torches are to hand when entering tunnels and for use at night.

It is advisable to be able to swim when contemplating a holiday afloat. Non-swimmers and young children should wear life jackets. When walking along the side-decks hold the handrails on the cabin top.

Make sure that you know the position and method of operation of the fire extinguishers provided on the boat. Take a basic first aid kit with you including insect repellent. It is a good rule to spend the first night aboard making sure that you know where everything is, how emergency equipment works and reading the instructions or handbooks on essential equipment provided by the owner.

Tunnels

Canal craft should be equipped with a suitable headlamp for navigating tunnels. This should be trained slightly to the right to avoid dazzling oncoming steerers in wide tunnels. Torches should also be carried. Go dead slow when approaching other craft but do not stop in tunnels except in an emergency.

There are three tunnels on the Llangollen Canal: Ellesmere, 81 yards long; Chirk 459 yards and Whitehouses 191 yards. None of these is wide enough for craft to meet within but all have a towpath. Those heading upstream to Llangollen will find that the current in the canal has a noticeable 'blocking' effect and slows their passage considerably compared with heading down the canal.

Bridges

Height

Some of the arched bridges have little headroom between cabin roof and brickwork. Boaters, particularly those with roof-top passengers, chimneys and tall pipes, are advised to look well ahead and play it safe rather than sorry!

Lift Bridges

Although visually often attractive, these lift bridges, like low brick arches, have their own special hazards for navigators. If you line your boat up with the coping on the towpath side of the bridge, the roof of your boat should miss the bridge decking, but if the wind catches the boat, or the boat hits the coping and bounces off, you could hit your cabin. When approaching these bridges, never allow anyone to stand at the bows of the boat near to where the cabin might hit the bridge – several tons of boat travelling at up to 4mph could easily crush them between boat and bridge. Never attempt to get off the boat onto the deck of a moveable bridge, this has proved fatal several times.

Use common sense when lifting or swinging the bridges and do not open the bridge if a vehicle is approaching. Where no gate is provided, a member of your crew should warn road traffic.

Most lift bridges are operated by the use of a windlass. Exceptions are at Wrenbury (Bridge 20) which is electrically operated using the standard BW Yale-type key (see page 18 for operating instructions) and Wrenbury Church (19) and one on the Prees Branch (Bridge 1) which are the only surviving manually operated lift bridges; these require not a key or windlass but a crew member's weight to lift the bridge by pulling on a chain.

Note: Do not stand on the roof of the boat or anywhere along the gunwale nearest the bridge deck when passing under lift bridges and never attempt to get off the boat on to the bridge deck.

BW Sanitary Station keys

(Yale type)

It is essential to have at least one of these on board to gain access to Sanitary Stations and water points. Keys can be purchased direct from British Waterways (see Useful Addresses on page 12) and from most boat yards and marinas.

Mileage

Hurleston to Frankton Junction	29
Frankton to Llangollen Wharf	15½
Llangollen Wharf to Llantisilio	1¾
Frankton Junction to Gronwyn	7
Gronwyn to Newtown	28

Locks

Lock Dimensions

In canal parlance, the Welsh section of the Shropshire Union system is composed of narrow canals, meaning that the waterway, and more particularly the locks, were built to take the traditional narrowboat.

Ex working boats must take great care firstly at Hurleston bottom and second locks where frost damage has caused the walls to lean inward. 6ft 11in beam will probably prove to be the limit here. The bottom and second single locks at Grindley Brook will also need care but if you can negotiate Hurleston you will pass through these.

As each newly restored section of Montgomery Canal has been opened its channel has been found restrictive but a little gentle use soon irons out the problems and the locks are fractionally more spacious than on the Llangollen Canal. Today, the lock dimensions of both the Llangollen and Montgomery canals are:

Length	up to 72ft (21.9m)
Beam	up to 6ft 11in (2.1m)
Headroom	7ft (2.13m)
Draught	up to 3ft (0.91m)

Number of Locks

Hurleston to Frankton Junction	19
Frankton Junction to Llangollen Wharf	2
Llangollen Wharf to Llantisilio	0
Frankton Junction to Gronwyn	8
Gronwyn to Newtown	19
	(of which 2 infilled)

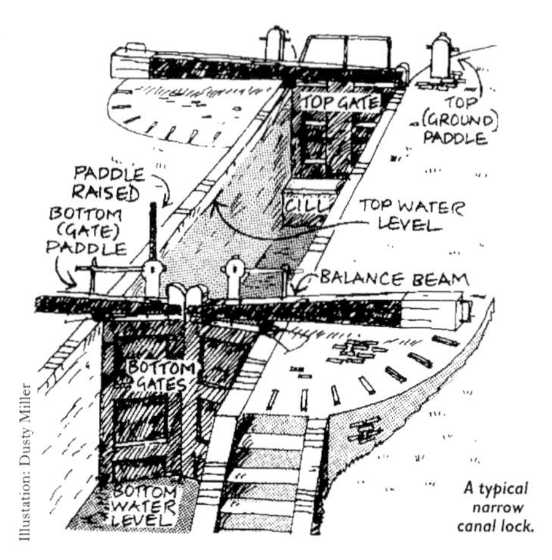

Illustration: Dusty Miller

A typical narrow canal lock.

Lock Operation

The golden rule is never waste water. The lock drill described below should be followed systematically.

The basic principle of lock operation is that water never passes straight through a lock. It comes in from the top and stays in, or goes out through the bottom without any following it from the top. If you liken the lock itself to a kitchen sink – the top end to the tap and the bottom to the plug – don't turn the tap on until the plug is in, and don't pull the plug out until the tap is off.

Lock Keepers The staircase locks at Frankton are only operable in the presence of the lock keeper. These are exceptions; lock operation on canals is usually undertaken by the boat crew. At busy spots such as Hurleston and Grindley Brook lock keepers may be available to assist and regulate traffic. They may ask you to share a lock with another boat or wait while another boat comes through the other way. Obey their instructions but do not necessarily expect that they will do the work for you – that's part of the fun of your holiday.

Staircase Locks Those at Grindley Brook and Frankton are the ones that concern us here. The staircase locks at Bunbury and the three-chamber set at Northgate in Chester on the Shropshire Union Canal Main Line are described in the *Waterways World* guide to that canal.

A staircase lock is one where the top gate forms the bottom gate of the next chamber. These abound on the Leeds & Liverpool where they are often referred to as 'risers'. Staircase locks are basically the same as ordinary locks and there is only one rule: When you're going up always make sure that the chamber above you is full (so that its water can be used to fill your chamber) and when you're going down check that the chamber below you is empty (so that the water from your chamber can be let into it). Only open the paddles between one chamber and one of its immediate neighbours at a time so as not to drain all the water from under your boat and do not try to empty a higher chamber into one below which is already full!

Several staircases have full-time keepers to assist, so look for notices advising of their presence and take instructions before doing anything.

How to Operate Locks

A windlass is usually required to fit the paddle spindles of manually operated locks. These will usually be provided on

Illustation: Dusty Miller

the boat and have two holes of different sizes to take the spindle's squared end. Take care to use the correct sized hole on the spindle as a bad fit is dangerous since the windlass may fly off. In direct contravention of the recommendation of its own paddle gearing committee British Waterways has fitted a mixture of sizes of spindles at numerous locks so constant attention is needed. Do not leave the windlass on the spindle when not winding the paddle up or down – make sure the pawl (or catch) is in place to stop the paddle falling and remove the windlass so that it cannot fly round if the catch slips.

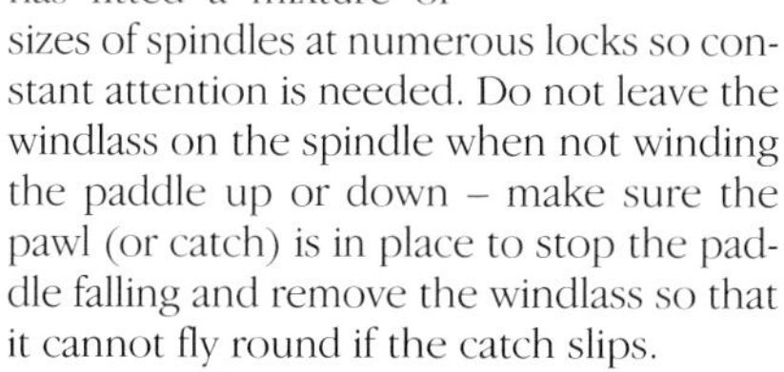

Those of the crew who operate the paddles must remember that the noise of the engine and rushing water will prevent people on the boat hearing their instructions, or them hearing shouts of panic. Those ashore are responsible for keeping an eye on the boat all the time that the lock is filling or emptying to see that it continues to rise or fall steadily. If there is any doubt, shut all the paddles quickly and then stop to think and check if the boat or its ropes and fenders are catching on any part of the lock or other boats. Particularly check that the stem fender does not catch under the top gate or its handrails when going uphill. Boats sharing locks, which is a good way to save water, must lie beside or ahead and astern of one another, *never* twisted across each other at bow or stern. Like that they will jam as the level alters.

(1) Going Uphill – Lock Empty

- Check that top paddles are closed.
- Enter the lock and drive the boat to the far end where there will be less turbulence as the lock fills.
- Close the bottom gates. See that the bottom gate paddles are closed.
- Open top ground paddles (where applicable). Water from these will pass under the boat to the other end of the chamber and hold the boat steadily against the top gate or cill.

Ropes are not usually required to hold a boat steady in narrow locks but will often be a good idea in bigger chambers. A line used as a 'spring' running slightly astern from the fore end may be best with some tension being maintained by keeping the engine running in forward gear. Do not tie knots in any rope used in locks, they will jam when it is necessary to adjust the length of line as the water rises or falls and leave the boat hanging in mid air or sunk. Do not try to hold a rope as the lock fills either; take a couple of turns round a cleat or bollard and the extra friction thus gained will help prevent the boat dragging the rope through your hand causing nasty burns as it does so.

Open the top gate paddles only when their outlets in the gates are submerged (where applicable). Some locks have only gate paddles and greater care is needed here to avoid flooding the fore end of the boat by opening these too much too rapidly when going up hill.

- When the lock is full open the top gates.
- Leave the lock. Close the top gates and all paddles.

(2) Going Uphill – Lock Full

- Check above the lock that there is no boat approaching that could save water by descending as you empty the lock for your boat to enter.

- If not, close the top gates. See that the top gate and ground paddles are closed.
- Open the bottom paddles.
- When the lock is empty open the bottom gates and close the bottom gate paddles. Proceed as (1) above.

(3) Going Downhill – Lock Full

- Enter the lock and drive the boat to the far end where it will be well clear of the cill near the top gates as the water drops.
- Close the top gates. See that the top gate paddles and ground paddles are closed.
- Open the bottom gate paddles.
- When lock is empty open the bottom gates.
- Leave the lock. Close all bottom paddles and gates.

(4) Going downhill – Lock Empty

- Check below the lock that there is no boat approaching that could save water by ascending as you fill the lock for your boat to enter.
- Close the bottom gates. See that the bottom gate paddles are closed.
- Open the top ground paddles.
- Open the top gate paddles when submerged (where applicable).
- When the lock is full, open the top gates. Proceed as (3) above.

Before leaving a lock see that all paddles are fully and securely closed. On canals it is important to shut the exit gates as well; failure to do so may result in serious flooding of property, stranding of craft through loss of water from the pound above, and possible flooding of craft when the pound is refilled.

It is easiest to pick up lock crew at the lock mouth, which saves approaching the shallow canal margins where you may run aground. But in all situations where crew are joining or leaving even a slowly moving boat make them get on or off at the stern. Should they slip they will then get wet after the boat has passed and not fall in where it will pass over them or crush them against a wall. At the stern the steerer is also at hand to put the engine out of gear quickly and assist.

Beyond The Towpath

This publication is intended primarily as a guide to the canal but it also includes information on some of the places of interest near the canal. More detailed information can be obtained from local tourist offices. (See page 12 and the text accompanying the maps for details of Tourist Offices).

Walking the Llangollen and Montgomery Canals

Although canal towpaths are not usually Public Rights of Way, the public is now encouraged to make use of these excellent long-distance footpaths. Some very good canalside walks may be enjoyed by combining lengths of towpaths with the official footpaths and bridleways marked on the appropriate OS Landranger 1:50,000 maps covering the area. Many of these tracks and byways are also marked on the maps in this guide. Cheshire's Sandstone Trail incorporates a short length of the Llangollen's towpath and the Offa's Dyke and Severn Way paths share that of the Montgomery.

The towpath will generally be found to be in excellent condition throughout. Bear in mind however, that, despite controversial 'improvements' in Llangollen, the towpath is not a tarmac path in your local park and strong footwear will be needed in rural areas. The bottom of cuttings can be wet after adverse weather. Whilst it is perfectly feasible to use the towpath as a long-distance traffic-free footpath, perhaps most will find more enjoyment from planning shorter 3–5 mile walks along lengths of special interest or scenic value, such as Chirk or Trevor to Llangollen or Hurleston to Wrenbury and across country to Nantwich to rejoin the towpath to Hurleston. Along the dry, infilled, section of the Montgomery Canal at Pant the path more nearly resembles an ordinary field path than a towpath and a few stiles will be encountered.

Where fences or gates cross the path, walkers should leave them as they find them.

Though 'lock-wheeling' is as much part of today's boating as it was in the days of working boats, it is an offence to cycle along the towpath without a permit. These are obtainable from British Waterways local General Managers' offices or from BW's Head Office. There are some lengths of towpath where cycling is not permitted, details of which will be sent to applicants along with their free permit, which must be displayed on handlebars at all times. Cyclists without a permit are liable to a fine.

Similarly, it is an offence to ride a horse along the towpath.

General

Always respect the pleasure of other waterway users and the life of the countryside generally. Do not litter or pollute the waterways and always observe the Country Code:

- Guard against fire risks.
- Fasten all gates.
- Keep dogs under proper control.
- Keep to the paths across farmland.
- Avoid damaging fences, hedges and walls.
- Protect wildlife, wild plants and trees.
- Go carefully on country roads.

Bibliography

The Canals of the West Midlands by Charles Hadfield. (David & Charles). An historical account, including the Shropshire Union system.

The Ellesmere and Llangollen Canal by Edward Wilson. (Phillimore, 1975). Historical background.

Narrow Boat by L.T.C. Rolt. (Republished Alan Sutton, 1994). Unequalled in canal literature. A 1939 voyage taking in much of the Shropshire Union Canal.

Landscape with Machines by L.T.C. Rolt. (1971). First part of autobiography. Includes the conversion of *Cressy* at Frankton in 1930.

Landscape with Canals by L.T.C. Rolt. (Allen Lane, 1977) Second part of autobiography. Includes *Cressy* on the Llangollen Canal in 1947 and 1949.

Towpath Guide No 4: Montgomeryshire Canal and the Llanymynech Branch of the Ellesmere Canal by John Horsley Denton. (Lapal Publications, 1984).

The Archaeology of the Montgomeryshire Canal by Stephen Hughes. (The Royal Commission on Ancient & Historical Monuments in Wales, 4th ed, 1989).

Thomas Telford by L.T.C. Rolt. (Longman). A full and readable, but long out-of-print, biography.

Thomas Telford by Bracegirdle & Miles. (David & Charles). An illustrated outline of Telford's engineering achievements.

Thomas Telford by Rhoda Pearce. (Shire Publications). An inexpensive paperback outlining Telford's career.

Thomas Telford's Temptation by Charles Hadfield. (M&M Baldwin, 1993). Examination of Telford's and Jessop's responsibility for the engineering of the Ellesmere and Caledonian canals.

William Jessop, Engineer by Charles Hadfield and A.W. Skempton. (David & Charles, 1979). The Ellesmere Canal's senior engineer.

Tales From The Old Inland Waterways by Euan Corrie. (David & Charles, 1998). Includes the life stories of Jack Strange, Llangollen Canal foreman who recounts the breaches of the Montgomery Canal and Llangollen feeder and Bill Dean, born at Weston Lullingfields Wharf.

The Montgomery Canal and its Restoration by Harry Arnold. (Tempus, 2003). A collection of historic and modern photographs.

Philippa Corrie

Obstruction Danger by Adrian Vaughan. (Patrick Stephens, 1986). Well-illustrated chapters on the Abermule collision alongside the Montgomery Canal and the breach of the Llangollen in 1945.

Severn Way Official Walkers' Guide by Terry Marsh and Julie Meech. (The Severn Way Partnership, 1999).

Waterways World magazine: many articles on various aspects of the Llangollen and Montgomery canals.

Maps and Charts

Ordnance Survey maps (Landranger Series) 1:50,000 scale: sheets *117 Chester, Wrexham & Ellesmere Port*, *118 Stoke-on-Trent & Macclesfield*, *126 Shrewsbury* and *136 Newtown & Llanidloes* cover the waterways described in this guide.

Waterways World Canal Guides to adjoining canals

At Hurleston Junction this guide links up with the *Waterways World Canal Guide 1: Shropshire Union*.

Other guides in the series

3: Trent & Mersey and Caldon (new edition 2005); *4: Grand Union – Birmingham to Northampton; 5: Grand Union – Northampton to the Thames; Oxford Canal; Kennet & Avon Canal; Coventry, Oxford and Ashby Canals*.

All are available from: Waterways World Ltd, 151 Station Street, Burton-on-Trent, Staffordshire DE14 1BG (01283 742970).

Useful Addresses

British Waterways General Managers

Llangollen Canal, Montgomery Canal and Shropshire Union Canal, north of Bridge 74: Navigation Road, Northwich, Cheshire CW8 1BH (01606 723800, Fax 01606 871471).

Shropshire Union Canal, south of Bridge 74: Albert House, Quay Place, 92–93 Edward Street, Birmingham B1 2RA (0121 200 7400, Fax 0121 200 7401).

British Waterways (Headquarters and Craft Licensing) Willow Grange, Church Road, Watford, Hertfordshire WD17 4QA (01923 226422, email: enquiries@britishwaterways.co.uk).

Web site: www.britishwaterways.co.uk. BW are also partners in www.waterscape.com.

Tourist Information

Ellesmere The Meres Visitor Centre, Mereside, Ellesmere, Shropshire SY12 0PA (01691 622981).

Llangollen The Chapel, Castle Street, Llangollen, Clwyd LL20 8NU (01978 860828, Fax 01978 861563, www.llangollen.org.uk).

Newtown The Park, Back Lane, Newtown, Powys (01686 625580, Fax: 01686 610065, email:newtic@powysgov.uk).

Welshpool Vicarage Garden, Church Street, Welshpool, Powys SY21 7DD (01938 552043, Fax: 01938 554038, www. visitwales.com).

Whitchurch 12 St Mary's Street, Whitchurch, Shropshire SY13 1YQ (01948 664577, Fax 01948 665432, www.stmem.com/whitchurchheritagecentre).

Canal Societies

Inland Waterways Association, PO Box 114, Rickmansworth, Hertfordshire WD3 1ZY (01923 711114, Fax 01923 897000; email: iwa@waterways.org.uk, www.waterways.org.uk/index.htm).

Friends of the Montgomery Canal, Inglefield, Four Crosses, Llanymynech, Powys SY22 6PR (email: friends@montgomerycanal.co.uk).

Shropshire Union Canal Society, 28 Millfield Drive, Market Drayton, Shropshire TF9 1HS (01630 656525, www.shropshireunion.co.uk).

Whitchurch Waterway Trust, Chemistry Farm, Chemistry, Whitchurch, Shropshire, SY13 1BZ (01948 662779).

Hire Boat Companies for the Llangollen Canal

Association of Pleasure Craft Operators, Parkland House, Audley Avenue, Newport, Shropshire TF10 7BX (01952 813572, Fax 01952 820363, email: apco@britishmarine.co.uk, www.britishmarine.co.uk). This is the trade association for hire and hotel boat operators.

Alvechurch Boat Centres, Scarfield Wharf, Alvechurch, Worcestershire B48 7SQ (0121 445 2909, Fax 0121 447 7120, www.alvechurch.com) have craft based at Wrenbury Mill.

Andersen Boats, Wych House Lane, Middlewich, Cheshire CW10 9BQ (01606 833668, Fax 01606 837767, www.andersenboats.com).

Anglo Welsh Waterway Holidays, Anglo Welsh Waterway Holidays, 2 The Hide Market, West Street, St Philips, Bristol B52 0BH (0117 304 1122, Fax 0117 304 1133, www.anglowelsh.co.uk) have a base at Trevor on the Llangollen Canal and bases at Norbury and Bunbury on the Shropshire Union Canal offering hire craft including one-way trips.

Black Prince Holidays, The Wharf, Stoke Prior, Bromsgrove, Worcestershire B60 4LA (01527 575115, Fax 01527 575116, www.black-prince.com), have craft based at Chirk Marina.

Chas Hardern (Boats) & Co, Beeston Castle Wharf, Beeston, Tarporley, Cheshire CW6 9NH (01829 732595, Fax 01829 730395, www.chashardern.co.uk).

Empress Holidays, Basin End, Nantwich, Cheshire CW5 8LA (01270 624075, Fax 01270 610274, www.empressholidays.com).

Maestermyn Marine, Ellesmere Road, Whittington, Oswestry, Shropshire SY11 4NU (01691 662424, Fax 01691 662424, www.maestermyn.co.uk) incorporates Maestermyn Hire Cruisers and Welsh Lady Hire Cruisers.

Marine Cruises, Chirk Marina, Chirk, Wrexham LL14 5AD (01691 774558, Fax 01691 773930, www.chirkmarina.com).

Middlewich Narrowboats, Canal Terrace, Middlewich, Cheshire CW10 9BD (01606 832460, Fax 01606 737912, www.middlewichboats.co.uk).

Viking Afloat, Wrexham Road, Whitchurch, Shropshire SY13 3AA (01948 662012, Bookings and general enquiries 01905 610660, Fax 01905 616715, www.viking-afloat.com).

Public Transport

Buses

National Express (nationwide service) (08705 808080, www.nationalexpress.com). The national Traveline (0870 6082608) will provide rail or coach information nationally and locally.

Trains

Times and fares are best obtained from the National Enquiry Number (08457 484950) or www.nationalrail.co.uk. There are stations at Chester, Chirk, Nantwich, Newtown, Welshpool, Whitchurch and Wrenbury. Llangollen's nearest station is at Ruabon (6 miles). There is a bus service from Market Street, Llangollen to Ruabon station.

Taxis

Details are most easily obtained from Taxi Line (0800 666666 or 0800 654321).

LLANGOLLEN CANAL

The Llangollen and Montgomery canals were part of a group of waterways administered by the Shropshire Union Railways & Canal Co. The modern Llangollen Canal, known familiarly as 'The Welsh Cut', joins the main line of the Shropshire Union system at the foot of Hurleston Locks. For details of the Shropshire Union Canal see the *Waterways World Canal Guide 1: Shropshire Union.*

Hurleston Locks

These four locks lead up to rich green Cheshire farmland, which is typical of much of the eastern end of the Llangollen Canal. This agricultural land is only lost to sight in cuttings. The canal remains in Cheshire until Grindley Brook where it enters Shropshire.

Behind the embankment alongside the locks is Hurleston Reservoir. The eight million gallons of water that flow down the Llangollen Canal each day from Horseshoe Falls at Llantisilio are stored here prior to treatment by North West Water for distribution as drinking water.

Bridge 1

Regular buses run to Nantwich and Chester along the A51. On the A51 near the bridge is Blackberry Farm, where you will find rare breeds of animals and birds, free range eggs, bedding plants and dried flowers, jams plus tea & coffee and ice creams – open 10am until dark in the summer months but at weekends only in the winter. A few hundred yards up the road is Snugbury's, a working dairy farm selling Jersey ice cream (24 varieties) (including ices suitable for diabetics) and frozen yoghurts, open 7 days a week, 9.30am–6pm in summer, winter: 11am–5pm.

Burland

A small village straggling along the main road. The Stores close to Bridge 6 can meet most of your immediate needs – groceries, hot pies, pet foods, liquor, cigarettes, sweets, papers, films – and is open every day (7.30am–6pm weekdays with half days on Tue & Sat and 9am–6pm on Sunday). There are phone and post boxes nearby.

Ascending Hurleston Locks at the start of a trip from the Shropshire Union Canal Main Line towards Llangollen. The lock house stands alongside the top lock in the background.

MAP 1
Hurleston Junction to Bridge 9

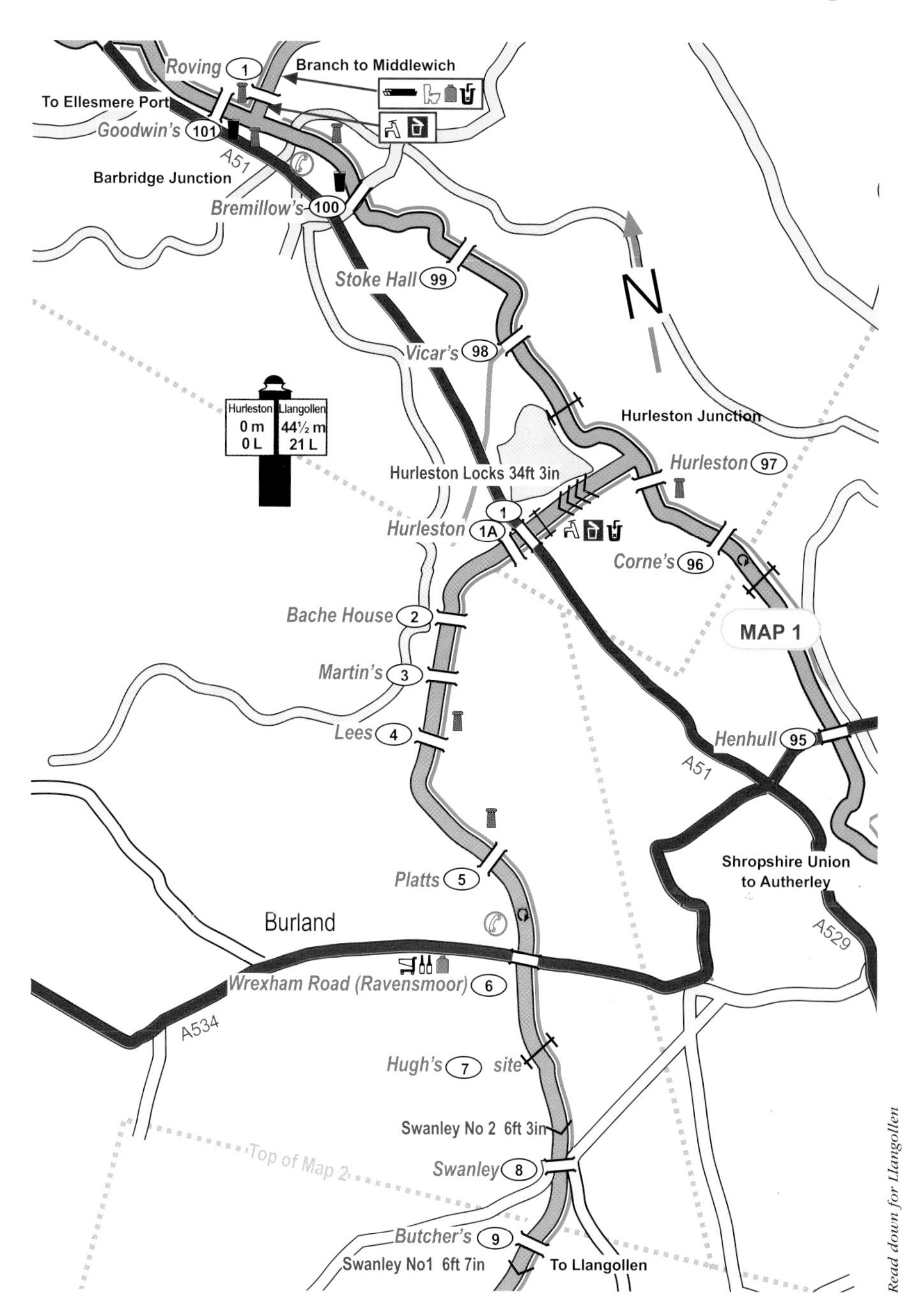

Read down for Llangollen

Ravensmoor

At the crossroads of this hamlet is the *Farmers Arms* (Greenalls, Flowers), serving home made bar meals and snacks to suit all tastes. There's a non-smoking dining room, beer garden, patio and play area, and the pub is open all day at weekends – best to book w/e meals in summer (01270 623522). Access is from Bridge 12 across a field path, or from Bridge 14 down the road. The general stores includes a newsagents and off licence.

Baddiley Top Lock – Bridge 17

A picturesque tree-lined stretch.

Wrenbury

Access to this conveniently situated village can be from any of the bridges between 17 and 20. Bridge 19 is closest (access by field path to the church), but Bridge 20 is nearer to the two pubs and the boatyard (note that the yard's services are not open to passing boats on Friday and Saturday, although emergencies are catered for). About five minutes walk past the pubs is the PO/village store which sells all the usual provisions, fresh fruit and veg, and has a deli counter plus coal, gas and papers (open 7.30am–6.00pm Mon to Fri, Sat until 4.30pm and Sun 8.30–1.00pm). There is a hairdresser next door and phone box across the road. Near to the canal, the *Cotton Arms* serves Tetley ales, bar meals and snacks and is open all weekend but for restricted hours in the week in winter. Overlooking the canal by Bridge 20 is the *Dusty Miller* (Robinsons), a former mill open every day all day from Easter to Oct and serving an extensive range of bar and restaurant meals every lunchtime and eve except Mondays (booking for eve meals during summer months advisable (01270 780537).

Although further from the canal than pubs which we normally mention in these pages the *Bhurtpore Inn* may be considered an essential entry by some canal travelers. This may have something to do with the eleven real ales normally on offer, the real cider, the Belgian, German or Czechoslovakian beers, the numerous malt whiskies, the excellent choice of home cooked food in the partly non-smoking restaurant or the beer festival held there in July. However, surely the real attraction must be the opportunity for an almost two-mile walk each way to Aston village from any of bridges 16 to 20! The pub is open (and serving food) every lunchtime and evening and all day on Sundays – booking for meals may be best (01270 780917).

Paradise Brewery (01270 780916), immediately beyond Wrenbury Station (a 20-minute walk from Bridge 20), is a micro brewery which was established in 2000. Tours are available between 11am and 4pm Mon–Fri and 12noon and 4pm at weekends when the licenced bar is open for those wishing to test the products.

The Church of St. Margaret has a finely decorated organ in a balcony and box pews with coats of arms on the doors.

Alvechurch Boat Centres (01270 780544; bookings and general enquiries 0121 445 2909, Fax 0121 447 7120, www.alvechurch.com). *(emergencies only Fri/Sat), showers, covered dry dock with hydraulic lift, repairs, souvenir shop. Open 9.00am–6.00pm, 7 days in summer. Hire craft including short breaks,* It's an attractive hire base in the converted mill by Bridge 20 once owned by Arthur Sumner, owner of a small fleet of narrowboats.

Bridge 20 This bridge is electronically controlled and requires a BW Yale key to operate. It is advisable to have two crew members on hand; one to man the road barrier and the other to operate the controls from a panel on the boatyard side of the bridge.

MAP 2
Bridge 9 to Wrenbury

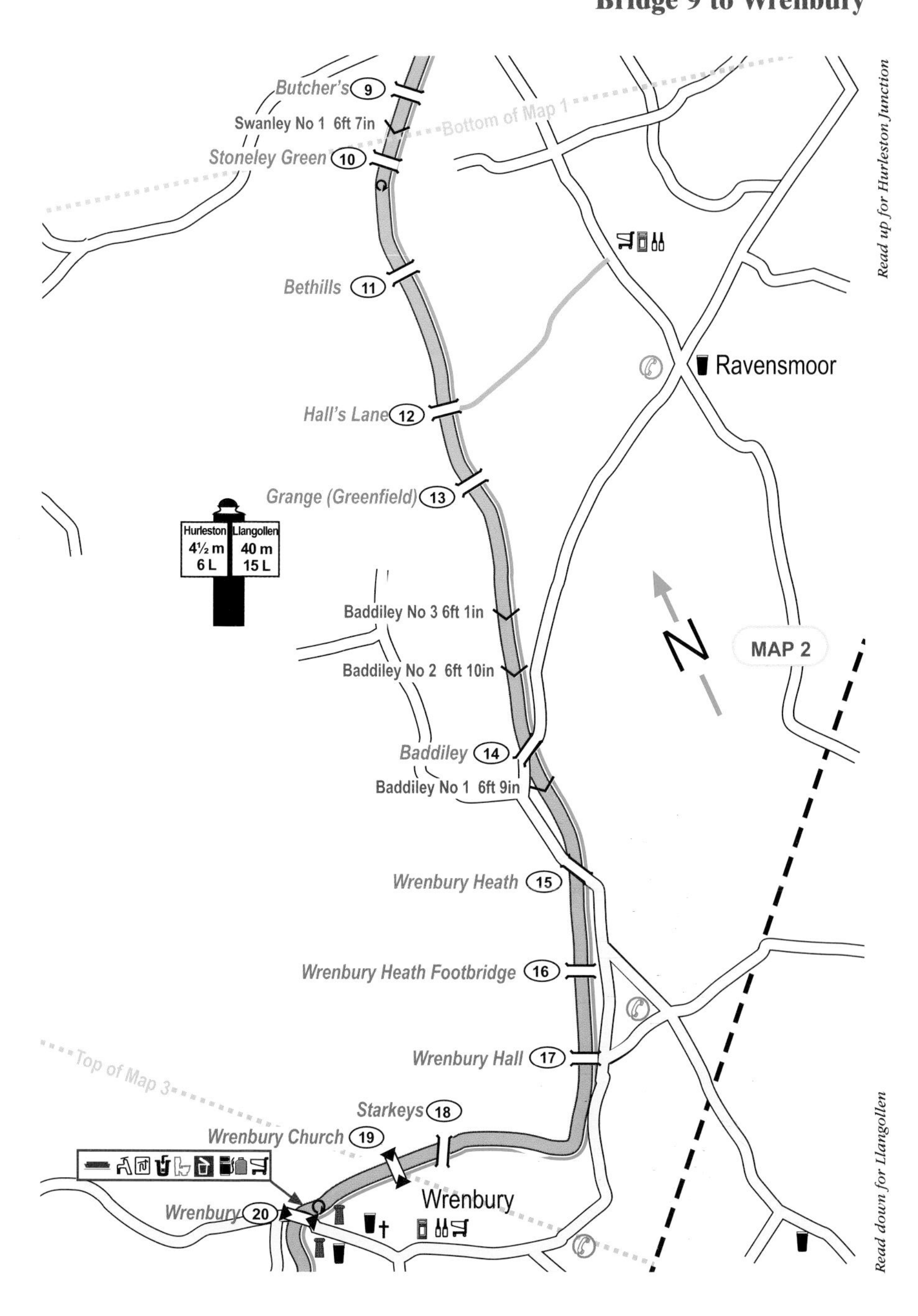

Bridges 21–22

The obelisk visible to the south is situated some 2 miles away in Combermere Park. Lift Bridge 21 is usually open.

Marbury *post box*

An attractive little village with small black and white halftimbered cottages. Access is from Bridges 23 or 24. *The Swan* (Pubmaster) is a typical country pub serving home-made meals and fish & chips to takeaway. There's a garden, and children and dogs are welcome.

Even if churches do not usually appeal to you, Marbury's Church of St Michael is well worth a visit for its beautiful situation overlooking Big Mere. It is particularly attractive in the evening with the sun setting over the mere, alive with wildfowl. Sunday services are at 10am and 6.30pm and the church is open daily to visitors.

Willey Moor Lock

From Willey Moor Lock to Grindley Brook Bottom Lock the towpath forms part of a trail devised by Cheshire County Council to show the main features of the sandstone area. The complete trail is 32 miles and crosses the Shropshire Union Canal's main line below Beeston Castle. *The Willey Moor Lock Tavern* (Free House, Theakstons and guests) has a licensed restaurant. It serves a choice of traditional ales and meals every lunchtime and evening. In summer it is advisable to book a table (01948 663274). There is an attractive beer garden and children's play area.

Wrenbury Mill Lift Bridge has been reconstructed; powered operation and a straighter road approach. As a result villagers complain about the speed of passing traffic and boaters must struggle with an awkward approach across the fore-ends of any Alvechurch boats that may project from their basin.

Waterway Images

MAP 3
Wrenbury to Bridge 25

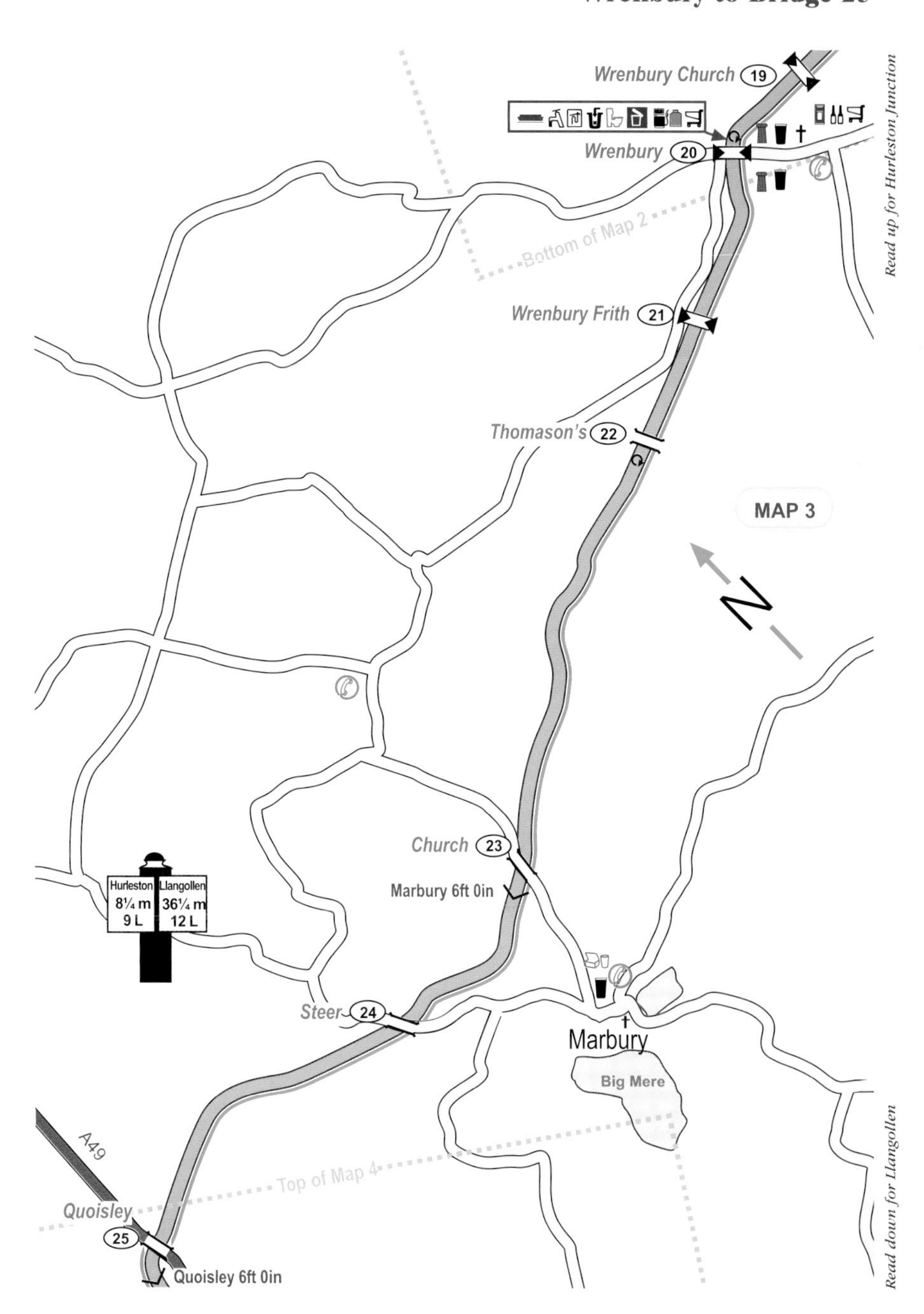

Waterwaylmages

The Telford-designed lockhouse commands the scene at Grindley Brook Top Lock.

Grindley Brook

(www.surftech.co.uk/GrindleyBrookVillage) Boaters intending to moor below the locks should do so on the visitor moorings before entering the short railway embankment tunnel. There are one or two useful, and some interesting, outlets here – down the road is the *Horse & Jockey* serving bar meals (lunch and evening). Just above the bottom lock is Grindley Brook Garage & Shop (access through a gap in the hedge) open 7 days and serving frozen foods, groceries, bread, milk, ice cream, solid fuels and logs, as well as engine needs. Also located by the bottom lock is Three Bridges Crafts (over Bridge 28), which sells cards as well as books and gifts during the boating season only. At the old wharf, is Buffy Robinson's Batik. Gifts of prints, cards, paper weights and bookmarks as well as plants and alpines. Upstairs in the Gallery are Buffy's original Batik paintings which may be seen by appointment only (March to October), (01948 665051). Alongside the staircase, Lockside Stores (01948 663385) can provide internet access as well as a coffee shop, snacks and fresh food, groceries and an off licence every day in summer.

Grindley Brook Staircase Locks

The top three locks are a staircase flight. For operating instructions see page 8. If you are still in doubt, ask assistance of other boaters or of the seasonal lock-keeper. British Waterways unfortunately deem it unnecessary to retain a full-time lock keeper in the splendid house beside the top lock, which Telford designed for the purpose. They are also responsible for the appalling destruction of the fine brickwork which had projecting 'scorchers' to aid the grip of iron-shod towing horses and for the suburban tarmac road which has replaced the historical stone surface of the towpath.

At the top of the staircase are visitor moorings with water taps and a launderette in addition to all the usual facilities.

MAP 4
Bridge 25 to Whitchurch

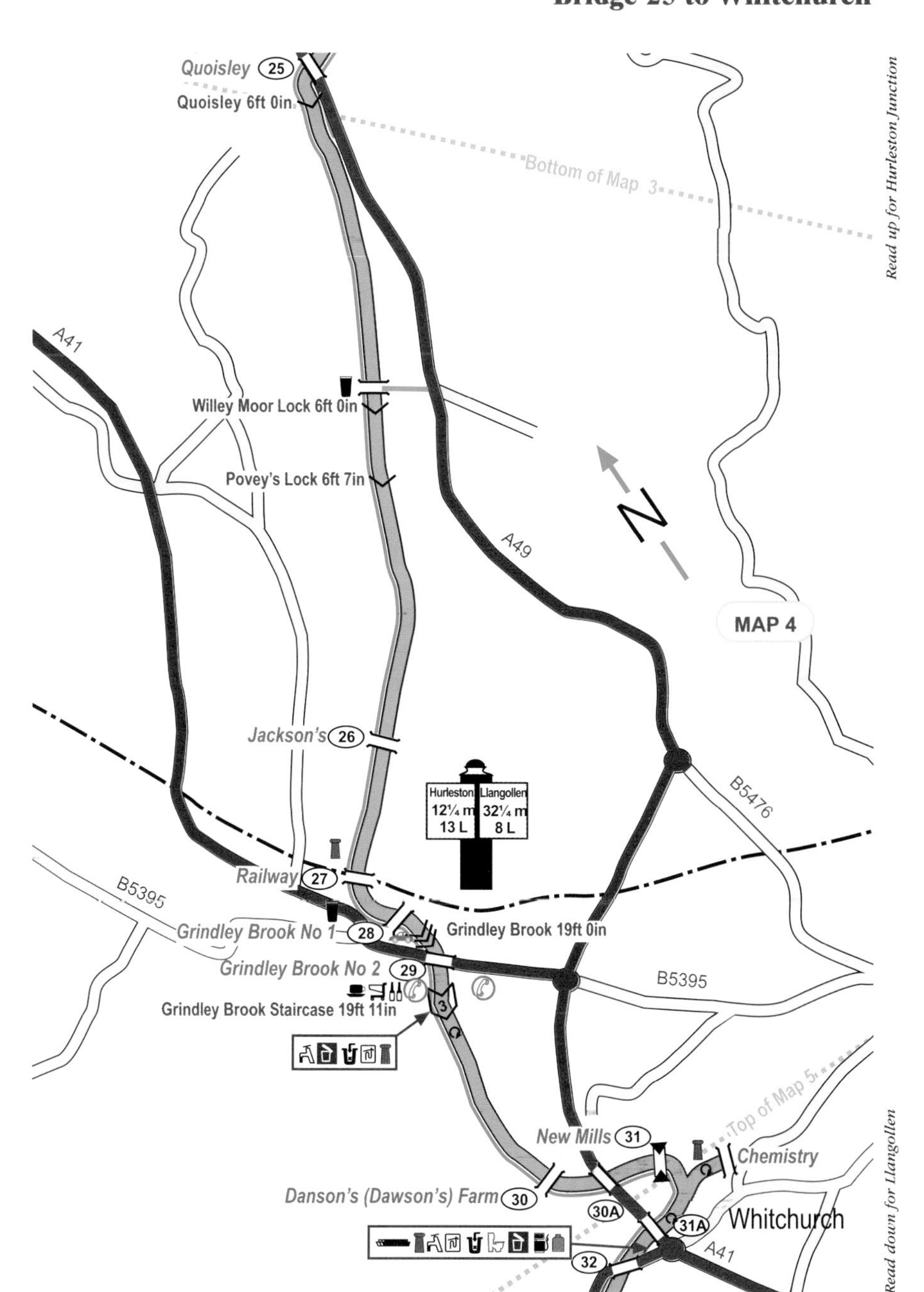

Harry Arnold/Waterway Images

The historical character of Grindley Brook locks has gradually been destroyed over the years as the brickwork which gave a grip for towing horses has been eliminated and the towpath converted into a road for motor vehicles since this picture was taken in the 1960s.

Whitchurch

All Services. Tourist Information Centre. Early Closing Wed, Market Day Fri.

Immediately south of Lift Bridge 31 is the former Whitchurch Branch Canal (or arm) abandoned in 1944 and infilled. But all is not lost, for today, thanks to the efforts of the Whitchurch Waterway Trust (see page 13), the first phase of work to re-open the arm towards the town centre is complete, providing visiting boats with a half-mile stretch to Chemistry Bridge, a winding hole and moorings. (Because the turning circle into the arm from the north – Grindley Brook direction – is limited, boats over 20ft can either reverse down the arm or turn in the winding hole 300 yards ahead by the by-pass bridge). The Trust's ambitious plans include constructing a new section of canal four metres below the original level (made necessary by a housing estate built on the old line), an inclined plane to transport boats to and from the new canal and a new town lake and country park.

Whitchurch, (20 mins walk from the present end of the arm) is a market town with interesting buildings and a variety of shops; it is also synonymous with Cheshire cheese – which may be sampled on market day (Friday) – and with clocks, namely Joyce's, that are still made here and can be found all over the world as well as in the tower of the parish church. The Tourist Information & Heritage Centre has displays of Joyce's work as well as others relating to the Romans and local artists and the usual timetables and reservations services. It also sells *A Pavement Safari – An Introduction to Whitchurch* by Richard Hughes which will bring to life some of the town's buildings and history for interested explorers.

Whilst Tesco has opened a superstore, there are still three family butchers, fish shops (including Shirley's Plaice in the High Street), bakers (including Walker's in the High Street who bake on the premises), delicatessens, including T.O. Williams, renowned for local cheeses, and a collec-

MAP 5
Whitchurch to Bridge 43

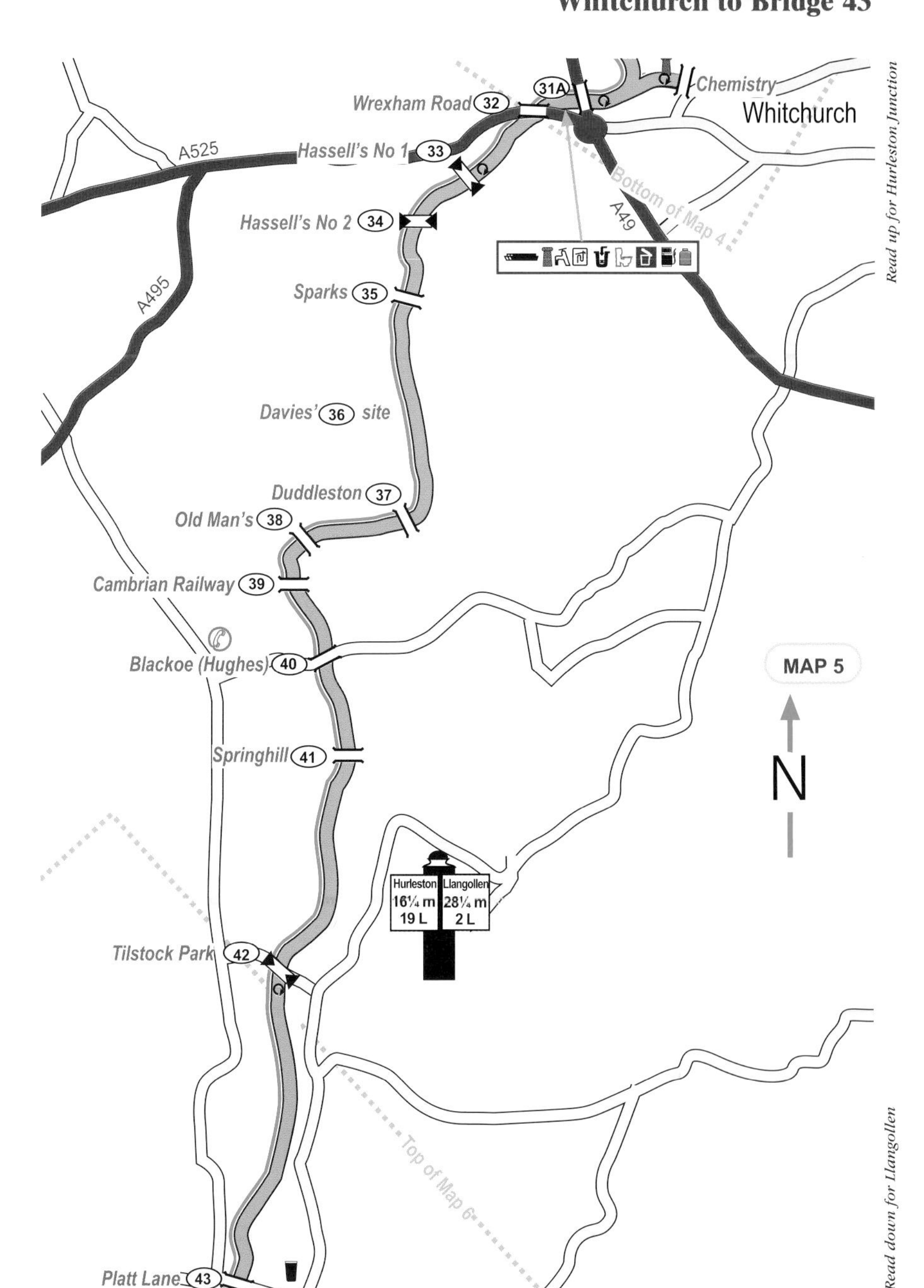

tion of useful shops in Watergate Arcade including a health food shop. There are banks, Indian and Chinese takeaways, restaurants including *Tolchards* (01948 662246, www.tolchards.com) a no smoking restaurant and pizzeria, which aims to 'offer terrific food and wine in informal surroundings' on Tue–Sat eves, and 26 pubs to choose from! You'll most probably find local Waterway Trust members in the *Fox & Goose* (Free House with changing real ales and food at all but Tue lunch and Sun eve meals) in Green End and in the *Old Town Hall Vaults* (Marston's) in St Mary's Street (open all day Sat with food every day) where the Trust holds its meetings. Among others are *The Greyhound* (which has B&B accomodation) in Bargate (food and pool table), the *Horse & Jockey* (Vaux) in Church Street (closed Mon but food at other times) and the *Black Bear* (Pubmaster) opposite the church (open evenings only except Fri–Sun).

Viking Afloat (01905 610660, www.viking-afloat.com). *shop (gifts, books, maps & guides), emergency repairs, moorings, hire craft, shower, caravan & campsite.*

Bridge 38 Notice the hole, occasionally still with door, in the face of some brick bridges. These were used for storing stop planks, which could be inserted into grooves in the narrows beneath the bridge in case of a breach or to drain the canal for maintenance.

Platt Lane

Two hundred yards from Bridge 43 (it's best to moor on the road side) you will get a warm welcome at the *Waggoners* (Free House with real ales) where home cooked food is served lunchtime and evening (bar meals, snacks or in the restaurant). Open all day, every day during summer, this friendly pub has a garden, pool table and other bar games and a payphone – best to book restaurant meals at weekends. (01948 880259). Back at the bridge, the red brick farm house sells quails eggs and produce in season.

Between bridges 43 and 44, on the towpath side, is The Barn, run by June Kemp. Open from May to September (closed Sat), the shop sells provisions, fresh milk, bread, fresh veg, Sunday papers, souvenirs, local crafts, maps & guides and has a payphone. There are good moorings on the towpath.

Bridges 44–47 (Whixall Moss)

A strange landscape greets the boater as you travel through this large area of peat bog. The 948 hectares of Fenn's, Whixall, Bettisfield, Wem and Cadney mosses are a Site of Special Scientific Interest and form the largest raised peat bog in Britain. It is unlike any other canalscape in England or Wales, but very reminiscent of the Irish peat bogs crossed by the Grand Canal. With its special flora and fauna, it offers great interest to the naturalist today, particularly if they are interested in insects, and is recognised as a Wetland of International Importance. Sixteen species of dragonfly alone have been recorded here, including the rare white-faced *Leucorrhinia dubia* dragonfly.

Access to the interior of the mosses is by permit only, obtainable from English Nature's Site Manager, Reserve Base, Manor House, Moss Lane, Whixall (¼ mile down the lane from Bridge 43) during office hours – please note that the office (01948 880362) is sometimes unmanned. You can reach the mosses either from Bridge 43 (by continuing beyond the office) or from Bridge 45, which is the main access point from the canal. At these points leaflets are available; these will act as permits for those walking only on the canal towpath and the main tracks through the mosses. Do not stray from these routes without a guide since there are many deep drains and areas of bog disguised by floating vegetation. Perhaps the best way to enjoy the environment of these mosses is by joining a guided walk organised by English Nature (see above).

MAP 6
Bridges 43 to 46

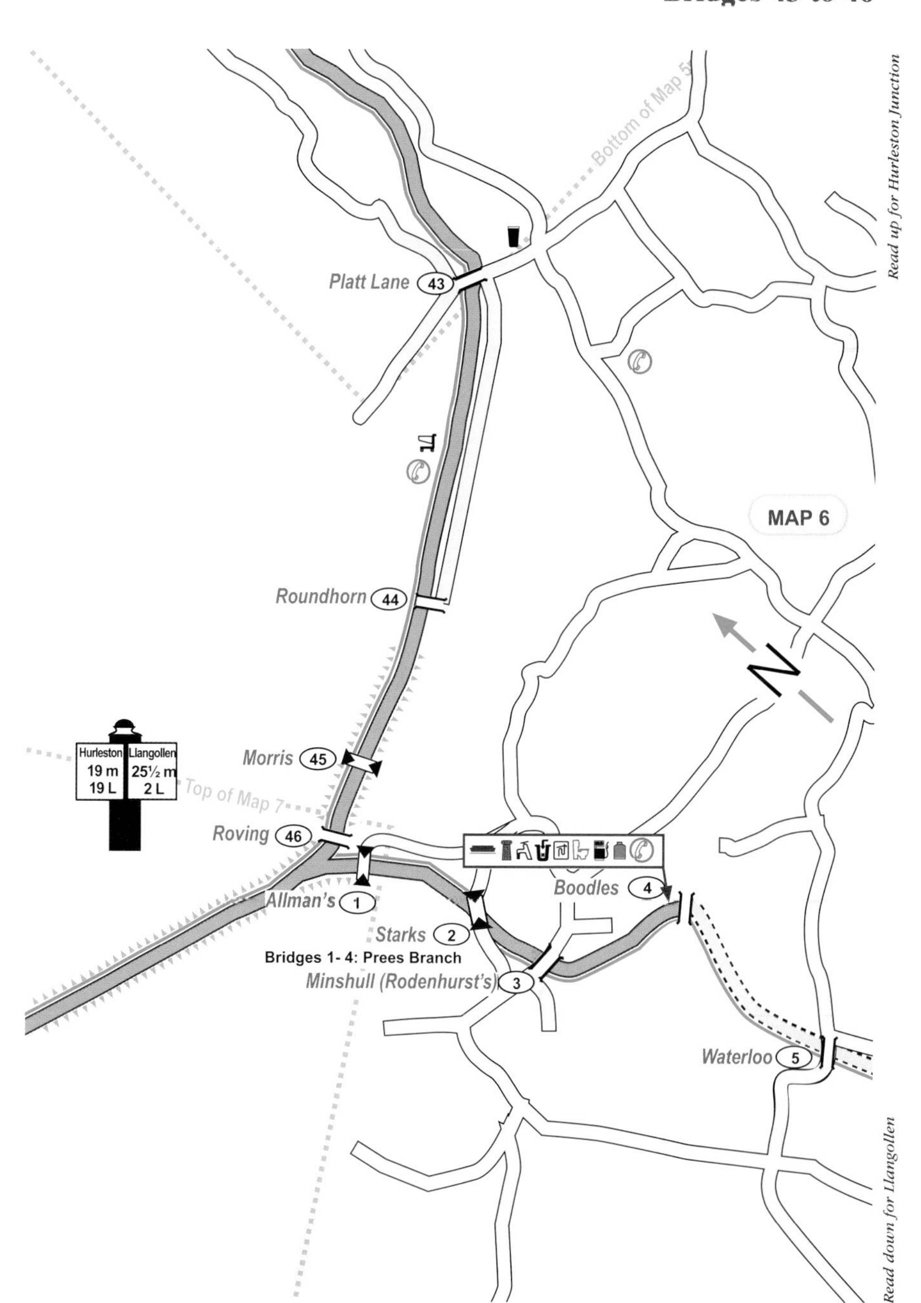

Prees Branch

This branch never reached Prees, but was opened as far as Quina Brook on the Whitchurch–Wem road by 1806. It was not built any further and limekilns were erected on the site. The branch was abandoned under the 1944 Act. The first mile (including 3 bridges, 2 of which require lifting) was reopened in 1974 to serve the marina which was constructed on the site of old clay puddle workings.

Whixall Marina (01948 880540, fax 01948 880420, www.whixallmarine.co.uk). *moorings, chandlery and souvenirs, solid fuel, wet dock, slipway, boatbuilding/painting/repairs/ breakdown service, boat brokerage.* Open 9.00am–5.00pm, 7 days.

Shortly after the junction with the Prees Branch, the canal enters Wales, the border having been close to the canal since Grindley Brook.

Bettisfield

The village has little to offer now as the pub, railway station and shop have all closed, but the church to the north is impressive on the hill.

Bridges 47–50

The length between Bridges 49 and 50 is a long embanked section. A mile and a bit east of Bridge 50 is the *Horse & Jockey* at Northwood, a 17th century inn serving meals lunchtime and evening and takeaway. Children and dogs are welcome, and a taxi service is offered back to the canal subject to availability, i.e. if they are not too busy!

Welshampton

This small village lies less than a mile from Bridge 51 – don't miss the sign-posted footpath across the fields close to the village which will save 10 minutes walk. At the garage, you can obtain mechanical assistance, while at the *Sun Inn* (01948 710637), you can be sure of wholesome home-made bar meals lunchtime (ex-Mon) and evenings all year round. There's a garden, payphone, cash machine and children's play area.

A widely recognised symbol of the Llangollen Canal – the rural lift bridge near Wrenbury Church.

Bridges 53–57

A beautiful and unusual section of canal passing through the Shropshire 'lake district'. Cole Mere stretches away below the canal to the south and, a little further on, Blake Mere lies on the other side of the towpath. Just before Bridge 53 is Lyneal Wharf where the Lyneal Trust (01743 252728, www.lyneal-trust.org.uk) provides holidays and canal boat trips for people with disabilities and with their families, friends or in groups on a specially adapted narrow boat or a day boat. The Trust also offers specially equipped holiday accommodation in cottages and chalets alongside the rural wharf. The Shropshire Lass, Shropshire Lad and Lyneal Wharf Cottages can be hired separately or in combinations together, by anyone with a disability, and their family and friends. Standing above Cole Mere, further on, must be one of the most idyllically located houses (thatched) on the entire canal system!

MAP 7
Bridge 46 to Welshampton

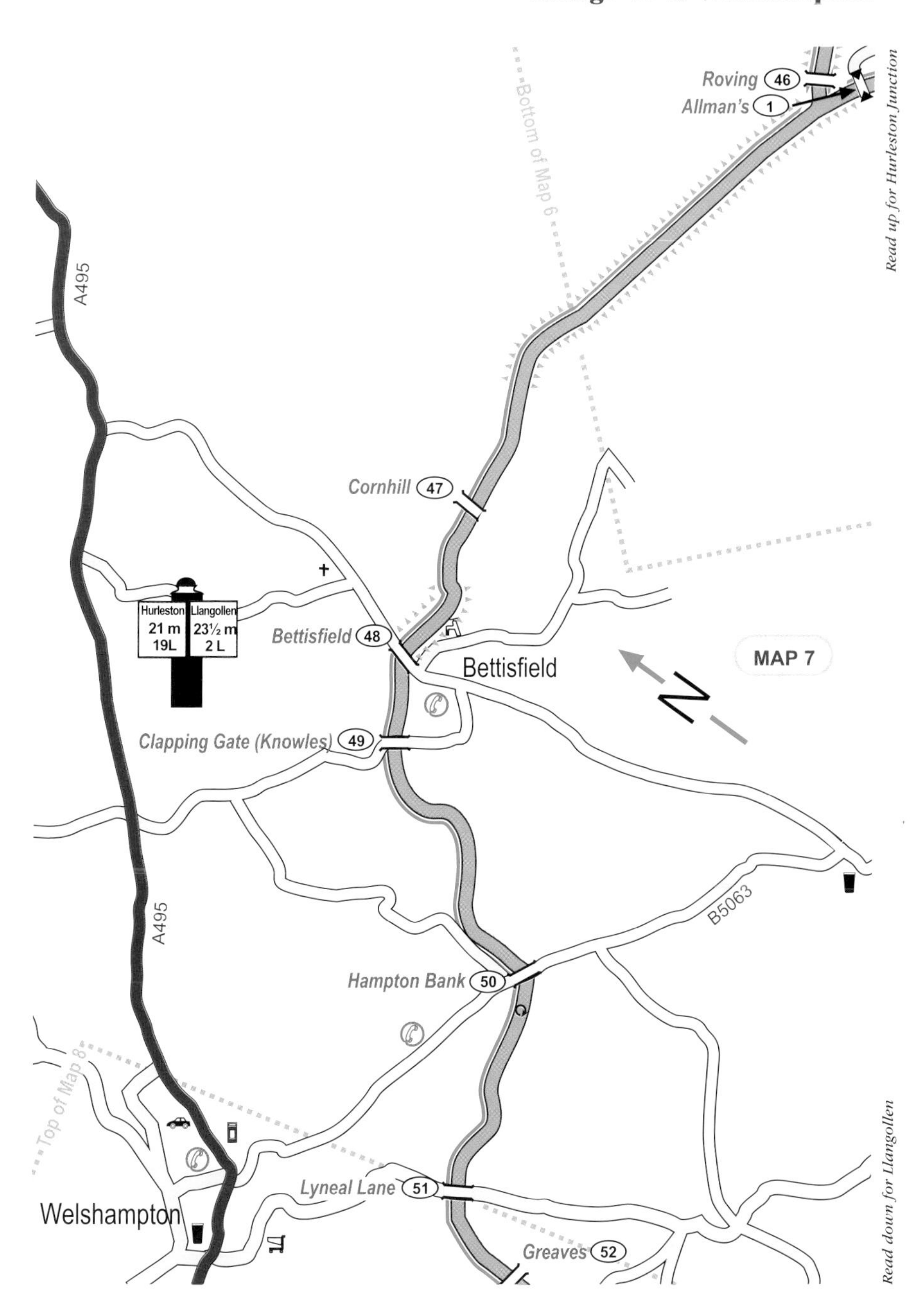

Ellesmere Tunnel (87 yards) A short tunnel with a towpath.

Blackwater Meadow Marina (01691 624391, www.blackwatermeadow.co.uk). *showers, chandlery and gift shop, solid fuel, slipway, engine reapirs and breakdown.*, Open daily 9.00am – 5.00pm ex winter Sun & Mon. Located between the tunnel and the junction with the Ellesmere Arm.

British Waterways Maintenance Depot (01691 622549). There are a number of interesting buildings here including Beech House (overlooking the junction with the arm) which was the HQ of the Ellesmere Canal Co, and a covered dry dock. For further BW details and the address of the British Waterways General Manager responsible for the Llangollen and Montgomery canals, see page 12.

Ellesmere

All services. Early Closing Thurs, Market Day Tue & Fri. A busy market town with a splendid Georgian Town Hall, complete with pedimented roof, and many period dwellings and shops. Moorings are available on the short arm or on the main line. It is possible to wind a full length boat with ease at the end of the arm provided that other boats do not tie up directly opposite one another at the extreme end. There's a small visitor centre in Wharf Road on the way from the arm into town.

Ellesmere is sandwiched between the canal and the Mere, where a Visitor Centre (open Easter to Oct, then weekends in autumn, 01691 622981) provides all you need to know about the meres and attendant waterfowl (the word 'mere' is Anglo-Saxon meaning lake). Refreshments are available at the mere-side *Boat House Café/Bar* throughout the year.

The town has a good selection of shops, many family owned, eating places and pubs. In Cross Street is Vermeulen's, an excellent delicatessen, notable for its fresh-baked bread and range of cheeses, B. Hawkins & Son family butcher, Beanstalk Health Foods and Pete's Sandwich Bar where snacks can be eaten in or taken away. In the Old Town Hall, in the High Street, is the *Cellar Restaurant* (01691 622433), which offers a wide variety of meals from roast dinners to soup and sandwiches. Also in the High Street is the *Ellesmere Hotel*, which welcomes children and offers bar snacks 7 days a week plus restaurant meals and accommodation. Nearby, *The Corner House* is a licenced non-smoking restaurant, which offers substantial and good quality breakfast, morning coffee, lunch and afternoon teas (closed Wed afternoon and Sun). There's a fish & chip shop opposite. At the *Black Lion* (Marston's) in Scotland Street they are proud of their *Good Food Guide* listing and serve fresh fish and vegetarian food as well as bar meals and snacks every lunchtime and evening. They also have accommodation and the Post Office is just along the street. The Spar shop opposite is open every day from 7am to 11pm. If it's fish and chips you want, then Mario's Plaice in Victoria Street (next to the launderette) will provide, but if you only require a drink, then try the *White Hart* (Marston's) in Birch Road, Shropshire's oldest ale house c1790 (open weekday evenings and all day at weekend). In the same street is the *Ellesmere Tandoori Restaurant* and takeaway (01691 623689).

The canal basin area has been threatened with redevelopment for several years with a combination of link road, industrial, craft and residential properties and plans to build a superstore where the old cheese factory stands, along with a pub and a wine bar in the former canalside warehouse.

Bridges 63–67

The canal takes a large detour around an outcrop of rock probably deposited here during the Ice Age. Around the apex of this bend are splendid views across the Shropshire Plain.

MAP 8
Welshampton to Ellesmere

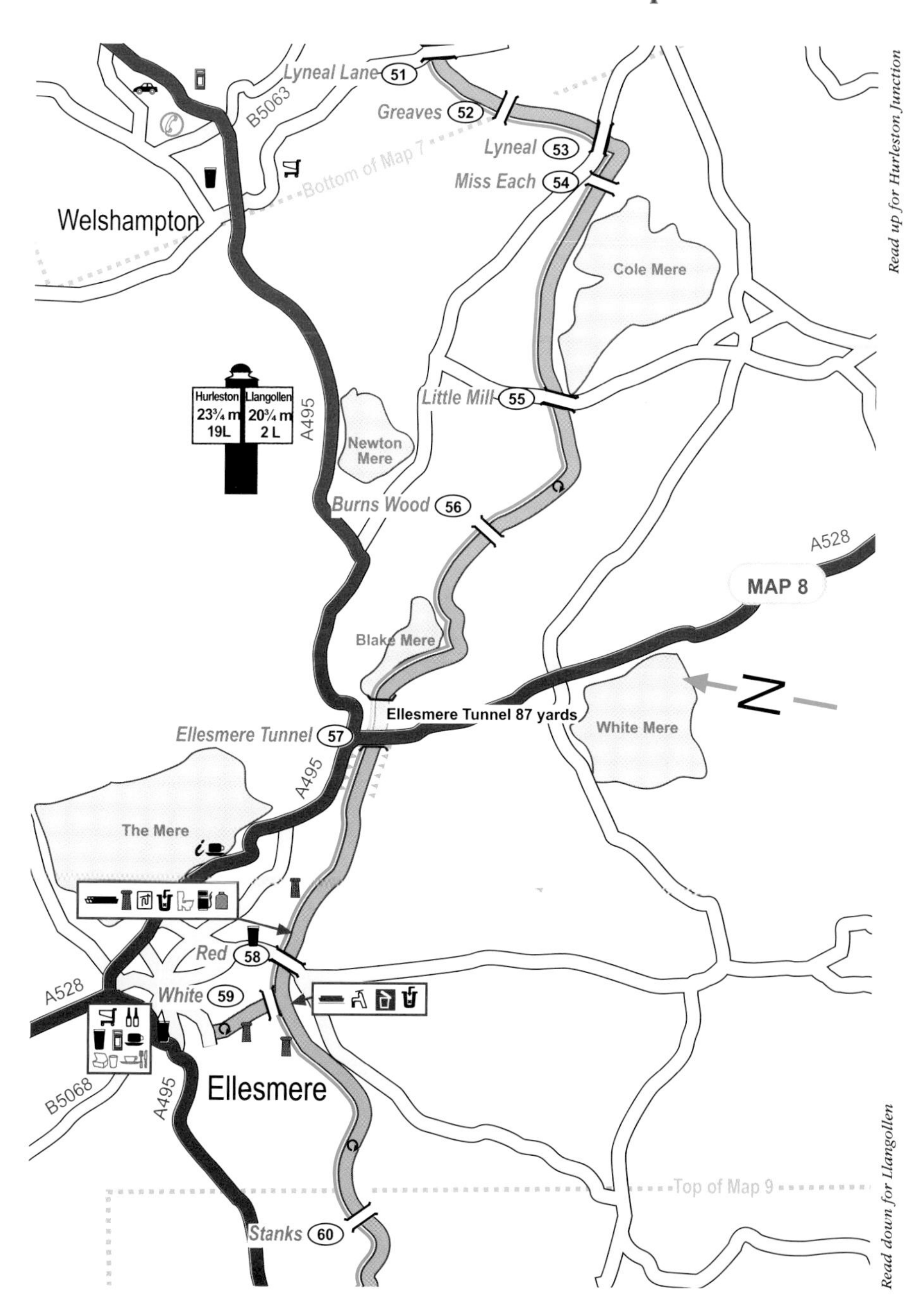

Philippa Corrie

The warehouse at the end of the Ellesmere Arm still proudly proclaims its former ownership.

Welsh Frankton ✆ *post box*

A walk up the steep lane from Bridges 69 or 1 to from the junction, which is at Lower Frankton, will lead to Welsh Frankton. The first hamlet consists of a few houses grouped around the canal and the second of a few more around the road junction.

Frankton Junction

The bridge numbers, which have run from 1 to 69, now begin again at 1 after the junction. The Montgomeny Canal (see page 44) branches off from here. The apparently illogical bridge numbering arises from the fact that the original scheme for the Ellesmere Canal was for a waterway from the Mersey via Chester and Frankton to the Severn. The section from Ruabon to Weston Lullingfields, a few miles below Frankton Locks, was completed before the company's financial problems stopped further construction. Later, attempting to make the best of a bad job, the water supply feeder from the Dee above Llangollen was made navigable and a new route from Frankton to Hurleston was cut.

Maestermyn Marine, Welsh Lady Cruisers & Shropshire Chandlers (01691 662424, www.maestermyn.co.uk). *chandlery and gifts, solid fuel, slipway for small craft, cranage and Boat Safety Scheme inspections can be arranged by appointment, boat building, fitting out, painting and repairs, breakdowns, hire craft, including day boats, and brokerage*. Open 9.00am–6.00pm every day.

The nearby *Narrowboat Inn* serves Tetley and guest real ales, bar snacks and meals (lunchtime & evening).

MAP 9
Bridge 60 – Frankton Juntion – Bridge 6

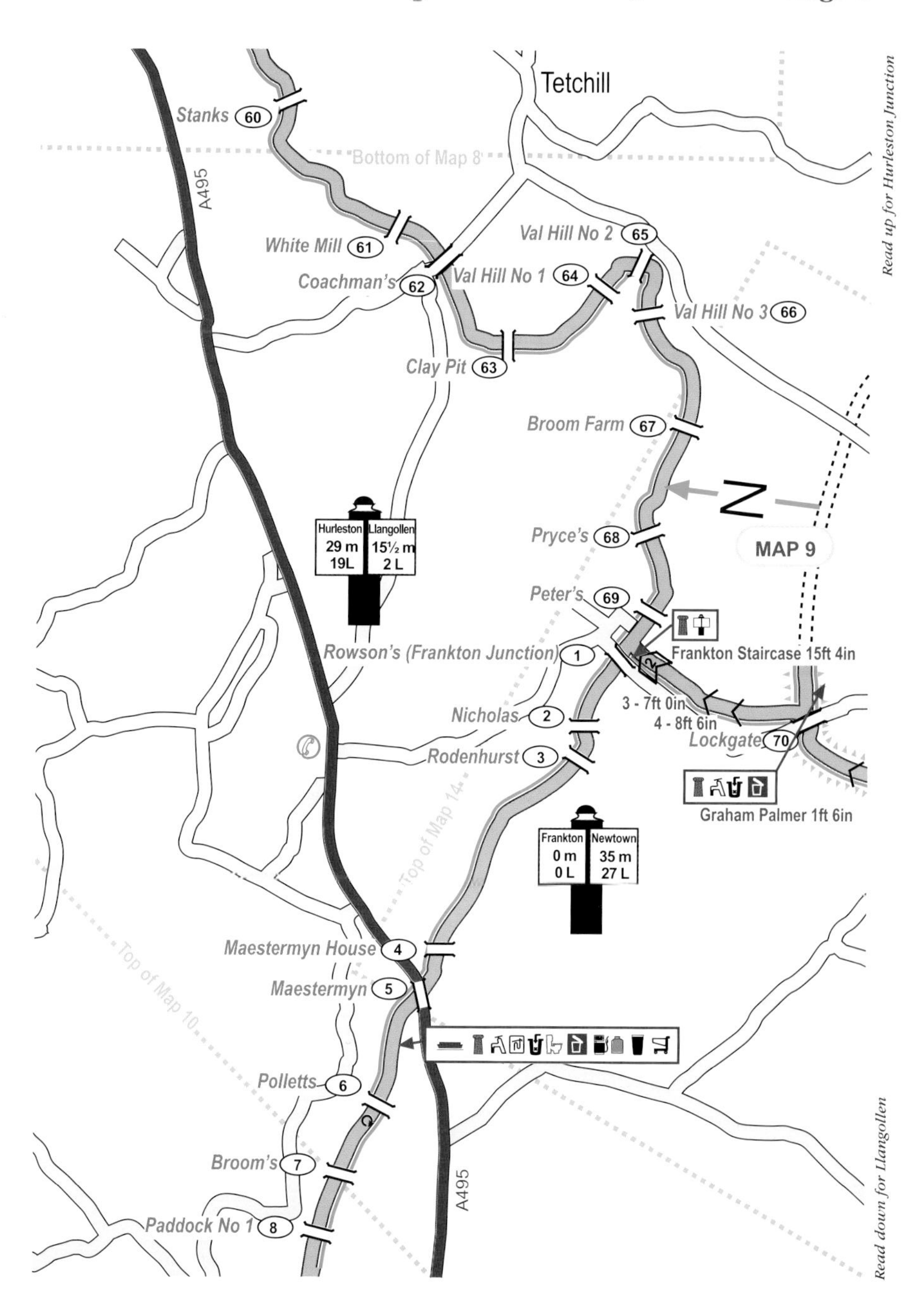

Euan Corrie

It is tempting to wonder if the builders of the Great Western Railway viaduct deliberately set out to overshadow Chirk Aqueduct with their modern all-conquering transport system.

Hindford

Just beyond Bridge 11 is the *Jack Mytton Inn & Restaurant,* which has a good reputation for its changing menus and serves real ales. It has ample canalside mooring and is open every lunchtime and evening, except on Mondays in winter.

New Marton Locks

There are no more locks between here and Llangollen despite the hilly nature of the area – another marvel of canal engineering. The water taps are now upstream of the bridge.

St. Martins

The village centre is about 1 mile north of Bridge 13 and has some interesting almshouses and a 13th century church with box pews.

Bridge 18

Seven minutes walk up the hill and over the level crossing is *The Plough*, a friendly Free House, where snacks are available all day, every day from an extensive menu. There's a dining room, games room and patio garden. The pub closes during the afternoon in winter but otherwise stays open all day. Booking for weekend meals advisable (01691 772536).

Bridge 19 – Chirk

The Poachers Pocket (Banks's) – formerly *The New Inn* – at Bridge 19 serves food (including vegetarian) every lunchtime and evening and is open all day Fri–Sun. There are moorings and a beer garden. There is a phone box close to Bridge 21 and down the hill on the old main road, the traditonal *Bridge Inn* (Cask Marque) offers Banks's real ale plus at least two guest ales and an extensive menu of meals (including vegetarian choices) throughout every day, which are made from fresh local produce. Booking is advisable at peak times on 01691 773213.

The canal here at Chirk Bank is high on the edge of the Ceiriog Valley with the old A5 down below. The 'new' A5 can be seen crossing the Dee valley by a high bridge. A sharp right bend after Bridge 21 (Bridge 20 has been removed but the narrows still remain) brings one suddenly on to Chirk Aqueduct with the higher railway viaduct alongside to the west. Chirk Aqueduct is constructed of 10 masonry arches supporting a stone-clad cast iron trough. Opened in 1801, it is 696ft long and carries the canal 70ft above the river Ceiriog, which forms the boundary between England and Wales.

Hindford to St Martin's

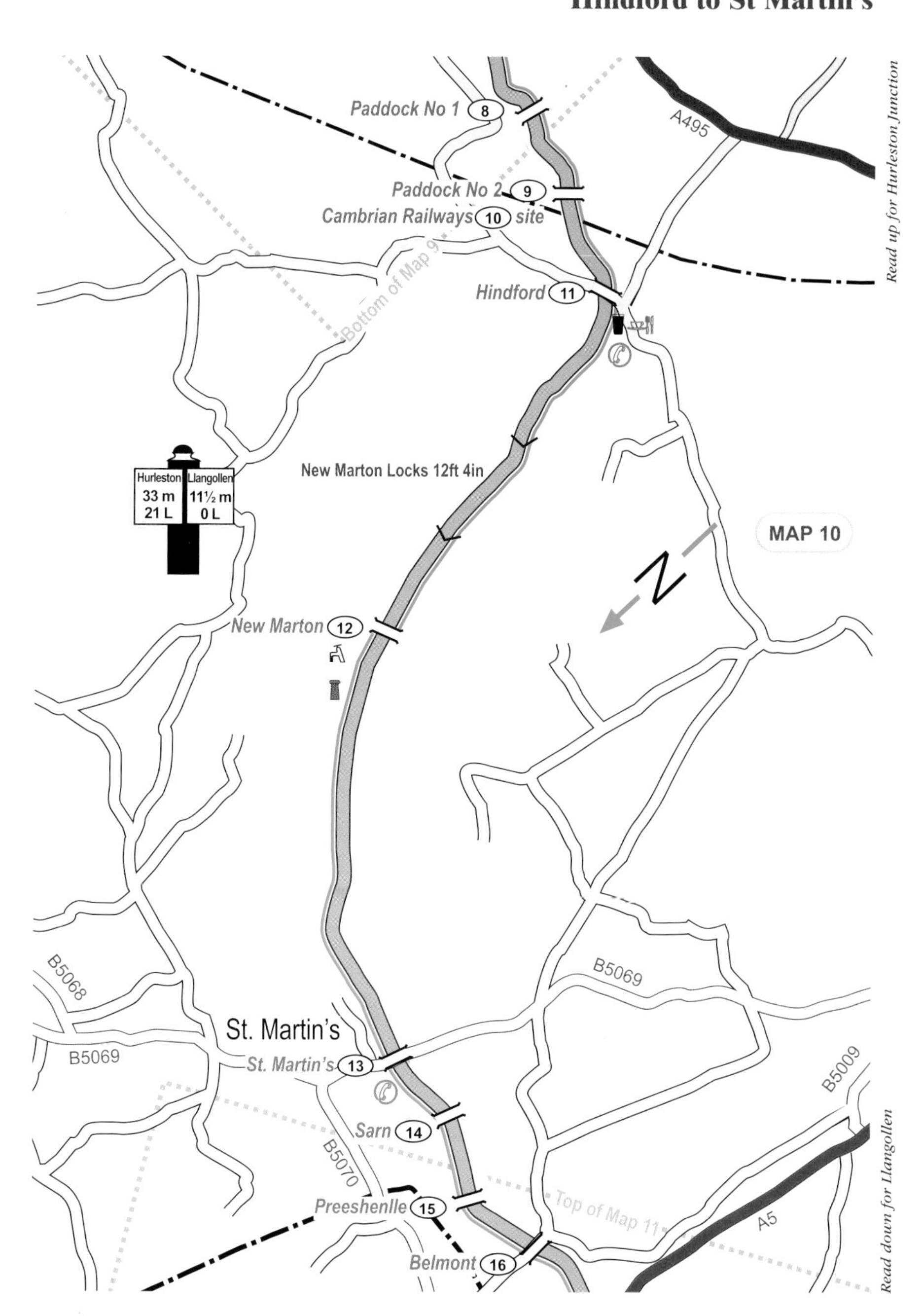

Chirk Tunnel (459 yards)
There's a towpath throughout this tunnel. The water is very shallow and progress against the flow will be very slow – similarly with the shorter Whitehouses Tunnel (191 yards).

Chirk

All services. The village is a short distance to the east of Chirk Tunnel. The roads at either end of the tunnel lead to the village, but there is more room to moor in the cutting upstream, or north, of the tunnel. Chirk is a compact village with a 12th century church and a few shops including a bank (Midland), Post Office, Co-op Late Shop and off-licence (8am–9pm ex Sunday 10am–4pm), butcher, chemist and newsagent. Eating out places include an Indian restaurant, *The Hand Hotel* (Tetley's) (01691 773472) offering home-made food lunchtime and evening, as well as morning coffee and afternoon teas, and the *Stanton House Hotel* (Free House) (01691 774150) which is more of a 'local' – it too offers meals lunchtime and evening and children are welcome.

Chirk Castle (01691 777701, www.nationaltrust.org.uk). Completed in 1310, the castle has a medieval tower and dungeon, state rooms, a long gallery, 18th century servants' hall and gardens. Open April to September on Wed–Sun, Bank Holiday Mondays and October weekends, 12.00–5.00pm (last admissions to park and state rooms 4.30pm). National Trust shop and tearoom (lunches & teas). At the tunnel, a notice states that the castle gate is only 400 yards away, which is true! However, be prepared for a further 1½ miles to reach the castle, a walk that is picturesque and well worth while through lovely 18th-century parkland which contains many mature trees and elaborate gates, made in 1719 by the Davies brothers. After 400 years of occupation, the house is still lived in by the Myddelton family. On the other hand, you may prefer to go by taxi, by telephoning for one from the public telephone at Chirk Bank or in the village.

By the winding hole beyond Chirk Cutting are the remains of a wall where transshipment facilities once existed with the Glyn Valley Tramway, a 2ft 4in gauge roadside line, which linked slate quarries at Glyn Ceirog, some 6 miles away, to the canal. Opened in 1873, the Glyn Valley Tramway was converted to steam in 1888 and re-routed through Chirk Castle estate to meet the Great Western Railway at Chirk Station. In the 1930s the quarries were closing or turning to road transport. Motor bus services soon brought about the end of passenger trains and on 6th July 1935 the last mineral train ran.

Chirk Marina (Marine Services) (01691 774558, Fax 01691 773930, www.chirkmarina.com). *chandlery, engine and boat repairs and breakdown call out service, hire craft* (operated by Marine Cruises, below). Overnight mooring is free and boat crews are welcome at the bar and restaurant, golf course (including club hire) and clay pigeon shooting.

Marine Cruises (at Chirk Marina) Offer 4–10 berth hire boats for short breaks as well as weekly hire.

Black Prince Holidays (01527 575115, Fax 01527 575116, www.black-prince.com) have hire craft based at Chirk Marina.

Bridge 16 – Chirk – Whitehouses Tunnel

Read up for Hurleston Junction

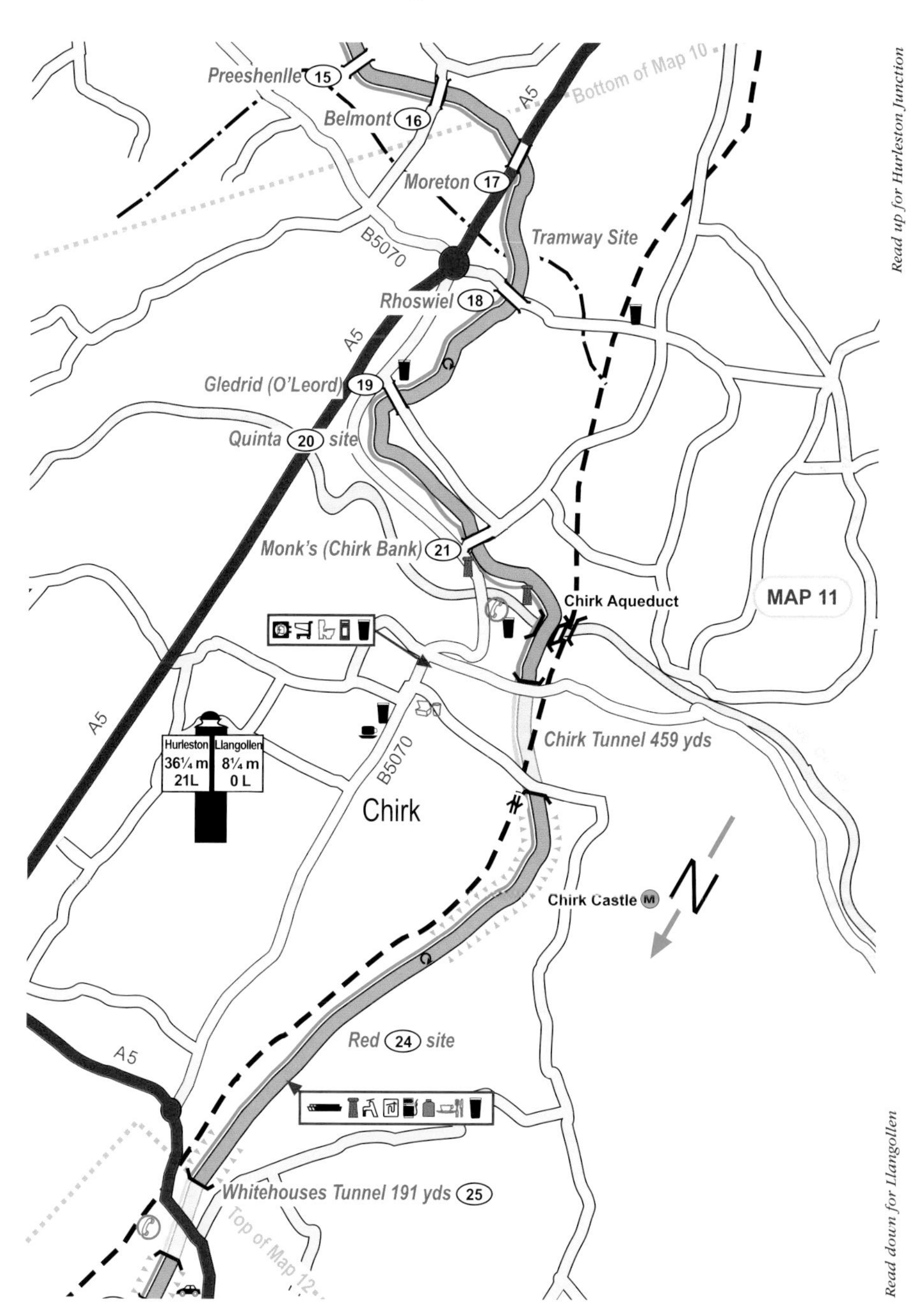

Read down for Llangollen

Whitehouses Tunnel (191 yards) is reached shortly beyond the marina and upstream passage is again slow.

Bridge 27 to Trevor

The canal runs high on the wooded side of the Dee Valley with glimpses of the famous Pontcysyllte Aqueduct and the railway viaduct through the trees.

Long sections of the canal between here and Llangollen have been rebuilt since the breaches of the feeder length. Most are of excellent depth, being built as a continuous concrete trough with imitation coping stones cast along the towpath edge. Lime kilns, once fed from the lane above, stand alongside the canal on the approach to Fron village.

The pump outlet by Bridge 28 is connected with the water supply to Hurleston. If more water is required to be fed down the canal from Llantisilio, or if the canal becomes blocked above this point for any reason (i.e. due to maintenance or a breach), pumps are switched on and can supply a similar quantity of water from the Dee 120ft below.

Froncysyllte

Access to the two pubs and PO/GS is either from Fron Lift Bridge (28) or up the wharf road beyond. The *Aqueduct* (Marston's) with its commanding view over the approach to the aqueduct, is open all day every day. The *Britannia Inn* (Free House) serves real ales, home cooked meals and takeaway, and has a games room and beer garden. Further down the road is the PO/GS providing basic provisions (open 9.00am–5.30pm Mon–Thurs, half day Fri & Sat closed for lunch 1.00–2 00pm).

Pontcysyllte Aqueduct

The *piece de resistance* of this canal, usually attributed to Telford, is this slender 19-arched aqueduct, 1,007ft long and carrying the canal 120ft above the river Dee. Its full story may be read in the books listed on page 11 – modern research suggests that whilst much of the design and the day to day supervision was Telford's, overall responsibility rested with William Jessop. There is a towpath with good railings on the east side, but only a few inches of cast iron on the other side – giving a strange feeling of floating through air high above the diminutive cricket players below. The aqueduct was opened in 1805, having taken 10 years to build. The masonry piers are hollow towards the top to save weight and support the segmented iron trough.

The later parts of the relining programme employed impermeable membranes with concrete walling as opposed to the all-concrete troughs constructed further upstream.

MAP 12

Whitehouses Tunnel to Sun Trevor

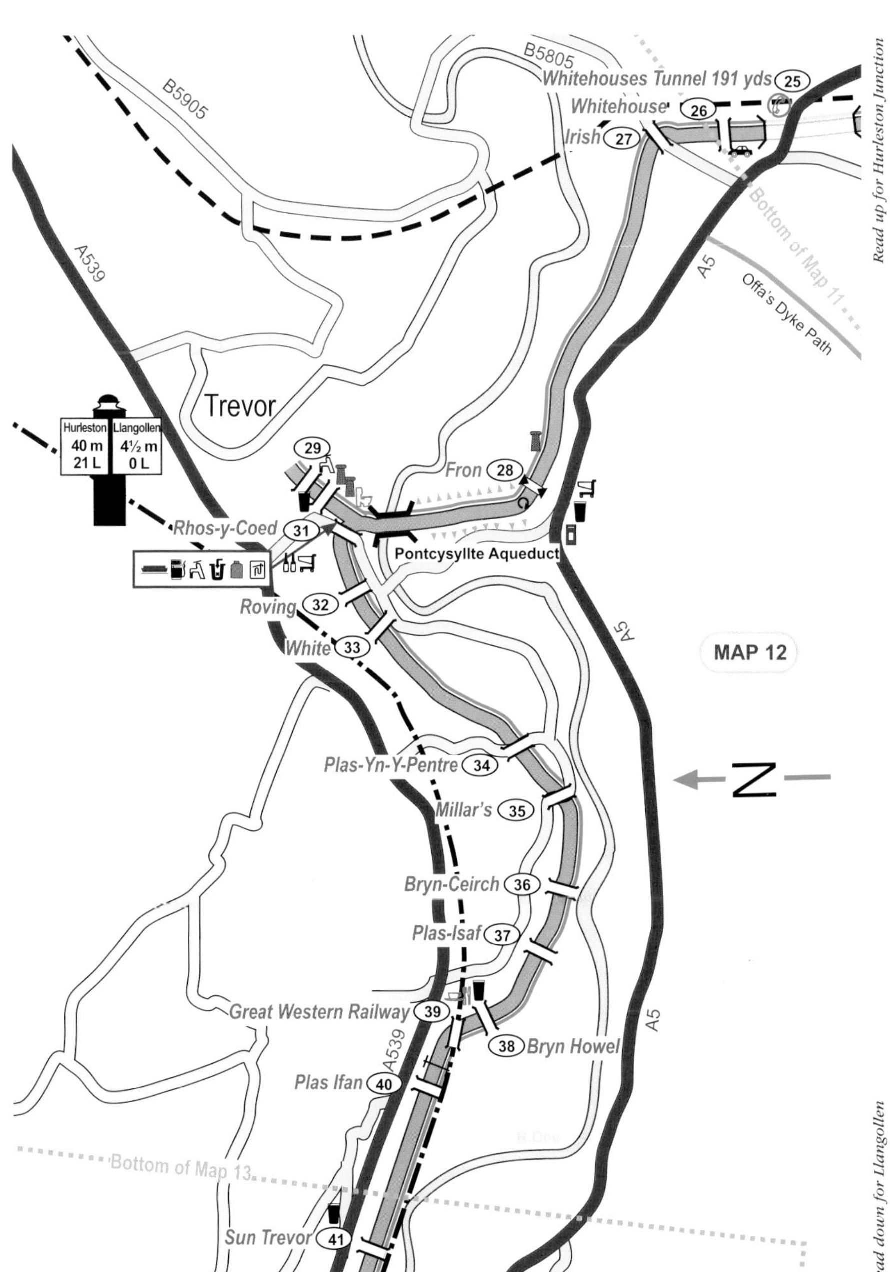

Pontcysyllte is certainly the high point of the Llangollen Canal and an icon of the engineering feats involved in building our inland waterways.

Maintenance of the aqueduct today presents certain difficulties, but none so great as must have been the construction of the huge spindly structure 200 years ago – a sobering thought. Indeed, there were originally plans to build three locks at each end so that a much smaller aqueduct could have been built.

Fortunately, confidence in late 18th century engineering techniques was sufficient to allow construction to go ahead at full height and we are left with a masterpiece unequalled on any other navigation anywhere in the world. There is a plaque celebrating the aqueduct's construction near the drydock at the Trevor end. The southern approach to the aqueduct is by a tree-lined embankment, the earth for which came from the deep cutting near Chirk Tunnel.

Trevor

There is a useful general store and off-licence on the housing estate behind the wharf (Trevor Wines & Provisions; Mon–Fri 8am–10pm, Sat/Sun 9am–9.30pm closed 1–2pm for lunch). Beyond the wharf (and accessible from the road only) is *The Telford* (Free House with Tetley's) open all day at weekend, and serving bar and restaurant food lunchtime and evening as well as all day at weekend. On the main road through the village is the *Duke of Wellington* with meals, games, quizzes, Sky Sports and a garden.

There are toilets in the car park close to the drydock. The canal beyond the Anglo-Welsh Boatyard is navigable for about 600 yards, and offers a quiet overnight mooring, a water point, and space to turn. This arm is all that was completed of the proposed canal to Chester. On New Road down Mill Lane from the bridge over this arm is the tiny *Mill Inn* where you might just find room to squeeze in. The industry on the hillside beyond (and clearly visible from the south side of the aqueduct) is Flexsys Rubber Chemicals (formerly Monsanto) Cefn Mawr Chemical Works. The works are a spectacular sight at night (and not too noisy); they are on the site of William Hazeldine's Plas Kynaston Foundry established around 1800 and responsible for some of the castings of the nearby aqueduct, the iron trough at Chirk, as well as castings for the Conway and Menai suspension bridges. The old buildings were demolished in 1946.

Boaters not wishing to proceed past Trevor can make use of a good bus service from the nearby main road to Llangollen. However, the 4-mile canal from Trevor to Llangollen should under no circumstances be missed.

Anglo-Welsh Waterway Holidays (01978 821749; bookings: 0117 3041122, www.anglowelsh.co.uk). *hire craft, chandlery, slipway, boat and engine repairs and breakdowns. Shop (gifts and canalware). Day boat hire and trip boat across the aqueduct.*

Trevor to Llangollen

The canal between Trevor and Llangollen is the result of a masterpiece of surveying by Thomas Telford, in that it clings to the contours of the hillside as it weaves its way towards its starting point at Llantisilio (a mile or so beyond Llangollen). It was built as a navigable water feeder, and in places is narrow and shallow (due mainly to rebuilding work following serious breaches in the 1940s and 1980s). Boaters should proceed slowly and carefully on this five-mile section to avoid damaging the banks; where the canal narrows and becomes one-way, be prepared to 'give way' to oncoming boats, restraint being the watchword! The *Bryn Howel Hotel* (01978 860331, www.brynhowel.co.uk) overlooks the canal and valley just upstream of Bridge 38. One of the Best Western chain, it offers full hotel, restaurant and bar services. Across the road from Bridge 41 is the *Sun Trevor* (01978 860651, www.suntrevor.co.uk) a Free House with a fabulous view across the valley. It offers bar food an *à la carte* menu and has a beer garden – there are mooring rings before the bridge.

This overhead view shows how narrow parts of the reconstructed feeder are, navigate with care and courtesy using the passing places to meet on-coming boats. Your return passage from Llangollen Wharf, with the current, will be much quicker than the upward journey.

Mooring at Llangollen

Mooring space at Llangollen during the peak season is at a premium. There are linear moorings between Bridges 44 and 45 and, in the summer of 2004 a new basin was opened just beyond the wharf above Bridge 45. You can either moor at the first available space after Bridge 44 or proceed through the last one-way stretch in the hope of finding a space closer to the town. The new 32-berth mooring basin with water and electric supplies helps to ease congestion. The maximum stay in the basin or on the towpath is 48 hours.

The basin and the towpath moorings in the town operate on a pay-and-display basis. Short stays of less than four hours and leaving before 4pm are free of charge, subject to availability. Other visits are charged at £5 per day. All boats will need to obtain a ticket from the British Waterways Customer Services Assistant at the information point by the facilities block on the linear moorings, east of Bridge 45.

(Monday and Tuesday are particularly busy at Llangollen when many hire boats arrive, so expect a degree of congestion.)

The limit of navigation for powered craft is at the last winding hole 300 yards beyond Bridge 45.

Llangollen Wharf

The Canal Exhibition, housed for years in the former Wharf warehouse, is now located at Llangollen Motor Museum up the road towards Horseshoe Falls. Today,

Hugh Potter

Llanddyn No 2 Bridge on the approach to Llangollen Wharf is a modern, hydraulic pump operated, reconstruction of one of the traditional Llangollen Canal lift bridges.

Sun Trevor – Llangollen – Horseshoe Falls

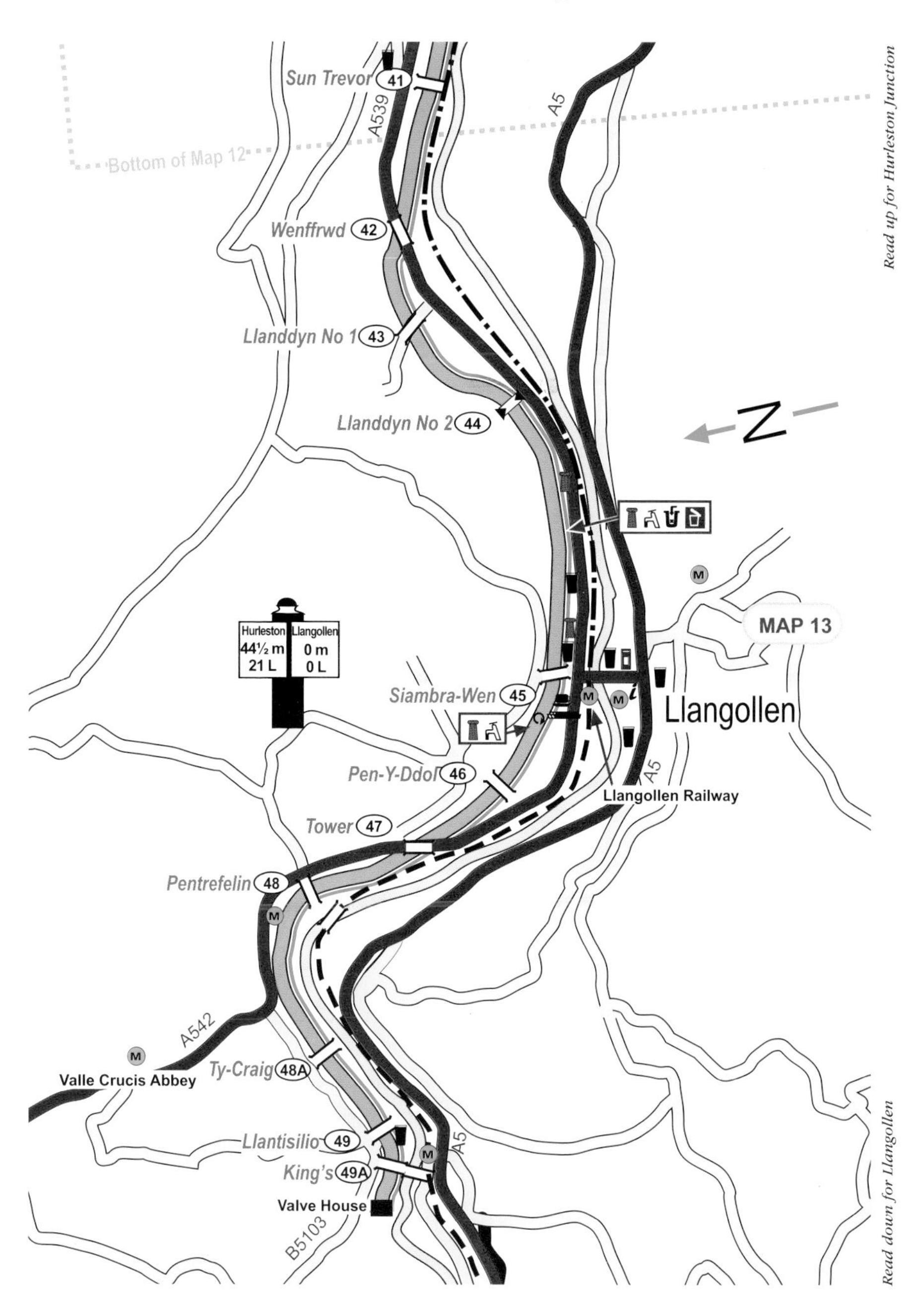

Llangollen's new mooring basin – opened in 2004.

Andy Talbot

in the Wharf building is a gift shop (open daily Easter to October 10am–5.30pm) and a cafe. Operating from the Wharf are horse-drawn boat trips (45 mins) along the tranquil stretch towards Llantisilio, and motor boat trips to the aqueduct aboard the narrowboat *Thomas Telford*. (01978 860702, www.horsedrawnboats. co.uk).

Llangollen Station The Llangollen Railway is based in the old station beside the river, where their locomotives are housed. The station is open throughout the year and steam trains run regularly during the summer. Trains run to the village of Carrog (where there is a tea room, pub and riverside footpath), giving a return journey of 16 miles – a trip not to be missed for its wonderful mountain scenery. (Talking timetable 01978 860951, other enquiries 01978 860979, www.llangollen-railway.co.uk). Combined rail/boat trips (up to Horseshoe Falls by train and return by boat, or vice versa) are also available on Saturdays during July and August.

Llangollen

All Services. Tourist Information.

Llangollen is famed for its International Music Eisteddfod held in July each year, when singers and dancers from all over the world converge on this picturesque little Welsh town (01978 862001, www.international-eisteddfod.co.uk). From the canal and its wharf, the town centre (largely Victorian) is but a few minutes walk down a steep incline and across the 14th century bridge over the river Dee. The Tourist Office, in the old chapel on Castle Street (see page 12), includes a gallery and hosts changing displays and exhibitions as well as dispensing guidance and information.

Facing the river bridge the *Bridge End* offers food every lunchtime and evening and earns a place in the *Good Beer Guide* for its Robinson's beers. Alternatively, along Mill Street towards Trevor is the *Ponsonby Arms* (01978 861119) that specializes in Thai cuisine and serves food every lunchtime and evening.

Shopping for food is well catered for and there are banks and gift shops as well as a good choice of eating and drinking places. Among these are the *Royal Hotel*, just over the river bridge, which has full hotel services and can offer meals from breakfasttime onwards all day, every day. *Gale's Food & Wine Bar* in Bridge Street (open 12–2pm, 6pm–10pm, closed Sun) offers an imaginative menu and an extensive wine list – children welcome. *Benson's Hotel*, opposite, serves Banks's, has accommodation and offers food, including brunch until 12 noon, as well as tea and coffee all day. The *Wynnstay Arms* (01978 860710, www.wynnstay-arms.co.uk) on Bridge Street has been in The *Good Beer Guide* for many years, being CAMRA Pub of the Year 2001, and offers Greene King, Abbot and Tetley beers as well as restaurant and bar meals every lunchtime and evening and hosts live jazz sessions. Then there's a cosy licenced bistro, *The Buttery*, in Market Street (closed Mon) offering hot dogs, sausage rolls, sandwiches and so on. *Books at Maxines Cafe* in Castle Street is a must for all book lovers – over 75,000 secondhand books are on display (open 10.00am–5.00pm).

Also worth a visit are Candlepower, on Castle Street, where you can see candles being made and have them personalised; the Old Tailors Chocolate Shop where the choice is vast and Paws teddy bear shop, where the inhabitants are newly made or repaired. The Post Office is close by and across Castle Street is a Spar grocers. Continuing on to Regent Street at the traffic lights will lead to the substantial *Hand Hotel*, which offers comfortable accommodation as well as full restaurant and bar meals service all day, every day. There is a launderette nearby as well as *The Gallery* Pizza Restaurant and Kwik Save. Real ale affectionados may find the walk from the wharf all the way to the *Sun*, even further along Regent Street, worthwhile for the changing real ales, real cider and food every lunchtime and evening. It is a past CAMRA pub of the year and hosts live jazz and folk evenings from time to time.

Plas Newydd This fine mock-Elizabethan house with its curios and elaborate woodcarving both inside and out is well worth a visit. Formerly the home of the eccentric 18th century 'Ladies of Llangollen', it is now looked after by the District Council and is open daily Apri–Oct, 10.00am –5.00pm; winter opening by arrangement (01978 861514).

Llangollen Motor Museum and Canal Exhibition About a mile up the road towards Horseshoe Falls. Open Tue–Sun, Easter to Oct. A collection of pre- and post-war cars and spares. This is now the home of displays from the Canal Museum, originally at the Wharf. (www. llangollen-motormuseum.co.uk, 01978 860324).

Victorian School A privately-owned re-creation of a Victorian schoolroom, open daily April to Oct, and at weekends all year 10.00am–5.00pm (01978 860794, www.victorianschool.co.uk).

Valle Crucis Abbey is about 2 miles up the A542 from Llangollen (leave the feeder towpath at Pentrefelin if you walk), but is worth a visit for its remarkably well preserved remains including the glorious west front, rose window and chapter house roof. It is in the care of Cadw (01978 860326, www.cadw.wales.gov.uk).

Llangollen to Llantisilio

The last winding hole on the canal is 300 yards beyond Bridge 45, which is also the limit of navigation for all powered craft. The only craft allowed beyond this point are the local horse-drawn passenger boats and unpowered craft. Mooring between Bridge 45 and the winding hole is not permitted. The 40-minute walk to the terminus, where there is a gauging station and valve house and the Horseshoe Falls (really a weir) at Llantisilio is well worth the effort, the Falls being the work of Thomas Telford. (About six million gallons of water pass from river to canal every day, most of it ending its journey at Hurleston 40 miles away where it is stored for eventual public consumption). Near the terminus is the *Chain Bridge Hotel* affording a breathtaking view over the river Dee. The hotel is open every day and all day throughout the year offering bar meals and snacks lunchtime and evening, and traditional Sunday lunch. Right by the river on Dee Lane is the *Corn Mill* (01978 869555) offering Boddingtons and Timothy Taylor ales and restaurant and bar meals all day every day. Over the road is a wide variety of crafts and wooden ornaments in The Market On The Fringe.

One other walk worth considering is to **Castell Dinas Bran**, an 11th century ruin on top of a 1,062ft hill (the one overlooking the canal as you approached Llangollen) and which gives spectacular views. Best access is via a footpath from Bridge 45.

Introduction

The general Introduction to this guide on pages 2–4 gives an overview of the Montgomery section's history and the bibliography (page 11) suggests some useful further reading.

The present Montgomery Canal and its 35 miles of largely rural meanderings are the subject of a major restoration project, begun in 1968 with the reopening of the section through Welshpool on its way to Newtown. The four locks at Frankton were restored in 1977 and a further 1½ mile section (including Graham Palmer Lock) in 1995. The canal was made navigable to Aston Locks (see page 48) by late 1996 but it was not until April 2003 that these locks were opened to navigation, extending the length connected to the main system as far as Gronwen Wharf.

Restoration

Work on the canal progresses slowly. In the 1980s an application to the then Secretary of State for Wales, Peter Walker, for further funds to complete restoration, was inexplicably refused. This despite the fact that officials in Brussels had stated that funding was already earmarked. Allowing local authorities, who had also reserved their own funds, to spend some £3m on the canal would have released £6m from Europe. There was much talk at the time of the British being too proud to apply for return of a proportion of their European community contributions, and of political pressures from the south Wales valleys in favour of other projects. Nevertheless, British Waterways, the local authorities and the voluntary organisations continue to work towards the canal's eventual full restoration which has simply been delayed, and not prevented.

In late 1993 Shropshire County Council began the first phase of a five-phase plan to restore the canal to the border with Wales at Llanymynech. Phase 1 was to build a new length of canal to the river Perry, including a winding hole, new lock and part of the Weston Arm. In conjunction with this, British Waterways did substantial work on the pounds between the locks at Frankton to ensure that they would hold water.

Phase 1 was completed in 1995 and officially re-opened in June of that year.

Phase 2 of Shropshire County Council's work began during 1995, and extended the connected cruisable length to 4 miles by late 1996. This includes a new Perry Aqueduct, re-built canal through to Queen's Head at a lower level (mainly to allow for lower peat ground level), re-built bridge to carry the old A5, and works to the other bridges on this length. The official opening was on 21 September 1996. This length is now available for cruising, subject to the availablity of the lock keeper to help boats through the two staircase locks.

Phases 3 to 5 will cover the length from Gronwen Bridge to Llanymynech.

Frankton Junction

If you do decide to cruise the re-opened section from Frankton Junction you can be assured of kind assistance and much helpful advice from lock keeper Colin Payne. The top two (staircase) locks are only manned for limited periods by Colin. BW are keeping the opening/manning times under review especially in the light of the re-opening of additional mileage beyond Queen's Head. Pre-booking is no longer necessary but for further information phone BW Ellesmere office on 01691 622549.

The bridge numbers, which have run from 1 to 69 up the Llangollen Canal, continue along the Montgomery Canal. This gives a clue that what we now call the Montgomery Canal, is in fact a continuation of the Ellesmere Canal's line to Carreghofa. Nowadays it is simpler to consider the waterway down Frankton Locks as a single entity – the Montgomery Canal – but its historical divisions are explained below as they occur.

Attractive, peaceful and rural moorings for those awaiting their turn to descend Frankton Locks onto the Montgomery Canal from the Llangollen.

There is space to tie up in the basin above the locks but you will often find it occupied by craft awaiting the limited opening times of the staircase. The empty area by the towpath to the east of the junction was once occupied by a wharf and warehouse with a hand crane to transfer heavier goods. Indeed this area was a complete and busy canal community with boatyard, cottages, pub and chapel as well as the wharf.

Frankton Locks

The top two locks form a staircase pair, but having read the instructions for working your boat through such locks on page 8 do not worry unduly since the lock keeper, usually Colin Payne, will be on hand when the padlock is absent and will give you careful and expert guidance. He is also a mine of information about the locality and this canal. A small toll house stands at the head of the locks and a plaque commemorates the restoration work here. By the top lock is a former stable and you should also pause to observe the wall alongside the towpath below the staircase pair. Such walls were normally avoided at all costs on a canal worked with long towing lines stretched from horse to boat but here the wall, which guarded those making their way up the steps to the pub, sports a curved rail to prevent the towline snagging. Pub? Unfortunately the *Canal Tavern* behind the towpath hedge is long closed.

The house on the offside below the third lock was once occupied by boatbuilder John Beech. It was at his drydock, now part of the garden, that the ex-Shropshire Union Canal Co horse boat *Cressy* was converted to steam power and fitted with a cabin for use as a pleasure craft. L.T.C. Rolt described in his autobiography his early trips on the nearby waterways with the boat's owner, his uncle Kyrle Willans. Tom Rolt subsequently bought *Cressy* and his account of his life aboard her, *Narrow Boat*, which lead to the formation of the Inland Waterways Association, has been in print continuously since publication in 1944. (Bibliography, page 11.)

Frankton to Bridge 70

The rebuilt canal chanel curves gently across the fields below Frankton Locks to a sudden T junction at Lockgate Bridge.

To the left would have been the main line to the Severn, had the Ellesmere Canal's promoters achieved their ambitions. Instead, the waterway ended at Weston Lullingfields, where some of the wharf buildings which originally included an agent's house, warehouse, cottages and limekilns survive. The branch was closed to navigation in 1917 but some Shropshire Union Canal staff continued to live in canal company houses at the wharf until the breach occurred in 1936. Most of what came to be known as the 'Weston Branch' is now dry, however it has been restored to navigation as far as the first 'narrows' (where a cottage once stood on the offside of the canal) to provide access to a sanitary station, water points and moorings.

To the right, through what motorists will expereince as a severely hump-backed bridge, is the route of the canal towards Newtown.

Bridge 70 to Queen's Head

Beyond Lockgate Bridge the canal runs slightly above a small stream. The low embankment, where the new side weir has been built, collapsed on the night of 5th/6th February 1936 draining the canal between Frankton and Aston Locks. Although the engineers of the time estimated that it would be possible to repair the damage for £400, the work was never carried out and eventually the whole 'Welsh' section of the Shropshire Union Canal was abandoned by Act of Parliament in 1944.

Since closure of the canal, drainage of the surrounding land has caused the peat bog to shrink and subside, reducing the level of the canal banks in the process. To compensate for this the canal's restorers elected to build Graham Palmer Lock and lower the water level to Aston. Graham Palmer was founder of the Waterway Recovery Group (WRG). This grew from a nucleus of members of the Inland Waterways Association to the present large organisation which calls upon sophisticated mechanical plant and large numbers of volunteer workers with a wide range of skills to undertake restoration work throughout the waterways.

Milepost number one (from Frankton) is passed as you set out across the moss. The iron mileposts – similar to those of the Trent & Mersey and Shropshire Union canals – that you will see along the towpath of the Montgomery, are not original here. Their provision has been organised by the Montgomery Waterway Restoration Trust and sponsored by various organisations and individuals. Not all are in place yet; those missing are intended for sites that will be affected by restoration works such as the future raising of dropped bridges.

The canal now strikes out across the peat moor to cross the river Perry by a concrete aqueduct where the original had been removed during the canal's closure. This low structure was really a group of culverts which obstructed the river's flow and the lowered canal bed would have made this problem worse had not the new aqueduct been designed with a single clear span. It is hard to imagine now that the whole of this length of canal has been redesigned – the original channel had no lining since, being cut into the peat bog, water tended to flow into the canal rather than out of it. A plastic membrane has had to be installed to retain the water which is now above the level of the surrounding water table.

In the early years of the 19th Century the canal ran part of its course across the

MAP 14
Frankton Junction to Bridge 74

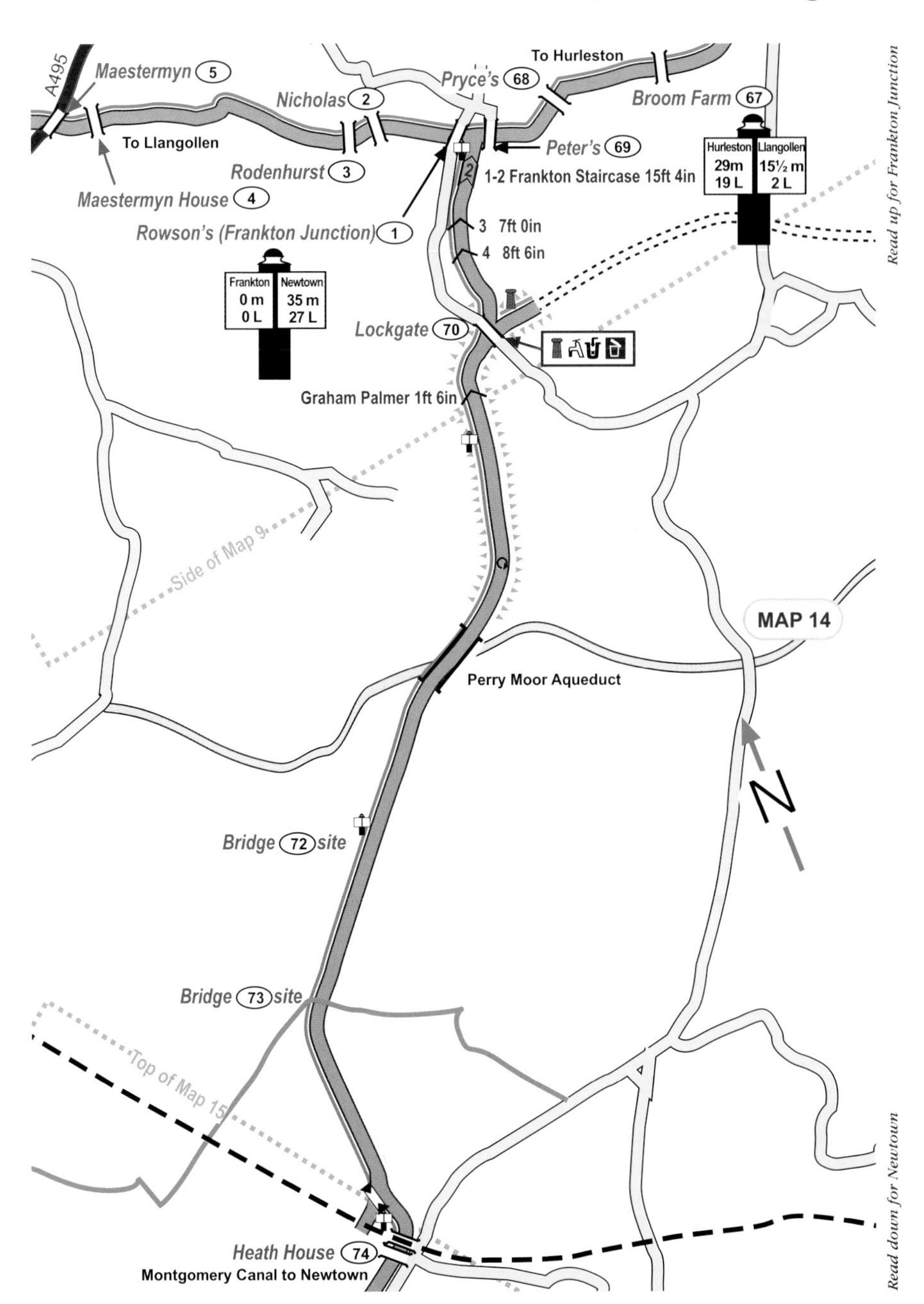

moss, towards Heath Houses Bridge a little north and east of its present route, to better serve the land owner's estate there before it was diverted to its present course.

A small swing bridge carries the towpath over the entrance to Rednal Basin, now a nature reserve. Here railway sidings allowed goods to be transhipped between the railway and the flyboats travelling to Welshpool and Newtown and there was a fertilizer works there until comparitively recently.

The railway bridge carries the former Great Western Railway line from Wrexham to Shrewsbury (the one which crosses the viaduct alongside Chirk Aqueduct).

South of the railway bridge a rebuilt, somewhat narrowed, canal channel leads past an attractive warehouse by the road. This was once a calling point for the flyboats providing express services between Ellesmere and Newtown. They provided a timetabled service and would collect and deliver all types of small consignments in much the same way as today's 'white van man'; skippers were instructed to stop to collect shipments by the use of a railway-like signal which can still be extended from the eaves of the building.

A straight section of canal alongside a busy minor road includes bridge holes, where the effect of lowering the water level from Graham Palmer Lock is very obvious, and leads to Queen's Head. Here is a winding hole and another warehouse where a tramway tunnel once extended beneath the road to enable easy loading of cargoes from the sand pit beyond. The *Queen's Head* pub has a good reputation for its home cooked bar and restaurant food (available from 12 noon every day) so that booking may be advisable (01691 610255). The menus change regularly, as do some of the real ales, although Theakstones and Old Speckled Hen are regulars.

One of the seemingly impossible obstructions to restoration of the Montgomery was the teeming traffic passing over the culverted remains of the A5 Trunk Road bridge at Queen's Head. However, in time, a new, larger, faster A5 was provided alongside the original. Building this gave the opportunity to remodel the minor road junctions and introduce a navigable bridge under the downgraded road to go with the one provided for the new carriageway. Not unnecessarily attractive, the two concrete spans none the less lead to increasing tranquility as one descends Aston Locks.

Aston Locks

Restoration of the next section of canal was subject to intense scrutiny in the interests of nature conservation. Despite the fact that the slowly silting waterway would not have remained as a man-made wetland without human intervention to maintain the status quo, the navigation restoration scheme has been required to fund extensive nature conservation measures. It is surprising to learn that the nature reserve alongside the top lock at Aston was, at the time of its construction the largest and most costly project ever undertaken by WRG. The bywash channel follows a winding course through the lagoons of the reserve to rejoin the navigation below the lock.

A walk up the field path from the middle lock leads to West Felton Village, astride the old A5, where *The Punch Bowl* (01691 601201) offers traditional food. There is a Post Office and Stores opposite.

Aston to Maesbury Marsh

The pleasant and peaceful rural canal from Aston Bottom Lock to Gronwen Wharf was opened to boats on 4th April 2003, almost five years after completion of the reserve.

At Maesbury Wharf boat crews may realise that the bridges of the Montgomery Canal are not always as high as those of the Llangollen section, so take care. To distract your attention from this hazard the *Navigation Inn* is close by on the wharf, which is overlooked by a Telford-style agent's house. Across the road on the wharf immediately downstream of the

Bridge 74 to Maesbury

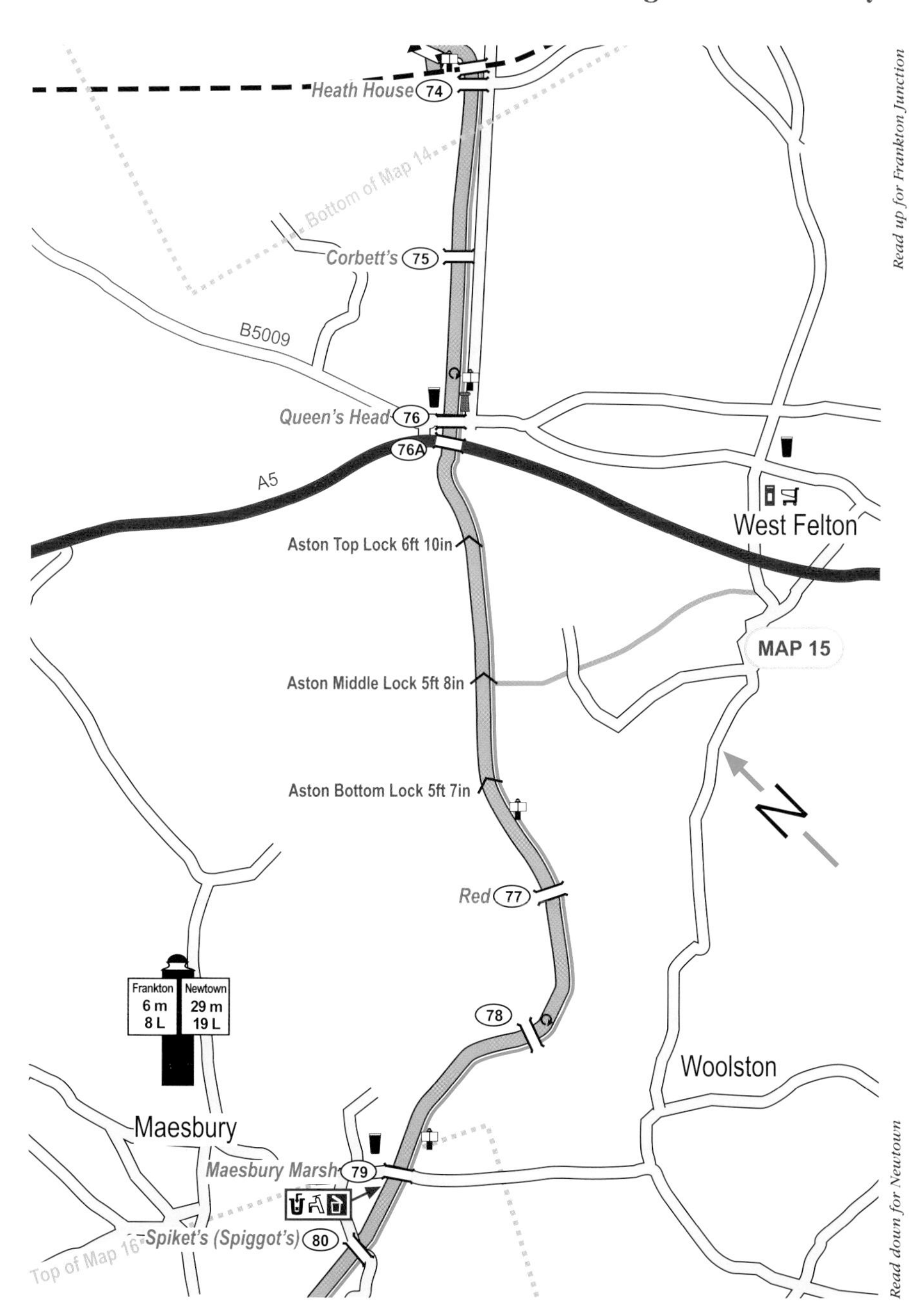

bridge a sanitary station was in the first stages of construction at the time of our visit and across the canal from that a farm sells fresh produce.

Near Woolston, half a mile from Bridge 78, is St Winifred's Well, which is named after a seventh century Welsh princess. The waters of the medieval well, which is the innermost of the three pools, are said to have healing properties, but access was closed to the public after users became too unruly – in 1755! It is now possible to stay on the spot in one of the Landmark Trust's smaller and remoter properties. (01628 825920, www.landmarktrust. co.uk).

Maesbury to Redwith

Beyond a new, windlass-operated, lift bridge are the modern industrial buildings on the site of A&A Peate's Mill. Peate's bought a number of the Shropshire Union Railways & Canal Company's boats when the latter ceased carrying in 1921 on the imposition of an eight-hour working day by the railway unions. Peate's continued to bring grain to their mill from Ellesmere Port and despatch flour until the introduction of motor lorries in the late 1920s. The majority of the older mill was destroyed by fire. Maesbury Marine Services now occupy part of the site and have restored much of the private mill arm.

Maesbury Marine Services (01691 679963, www.maesburymarineservices. co.uk) offer the full range of boat building and repairing services but have no facilities for DIY work. They can arrange independent Boat Safety Scheme inspections and cranage when required.

A few hundred yards further on Gronwen Wharf is reached. This became the end of the connected navigation from Welsh Frankton in 2003.

The wharf here was built as an interchange point with a four-mile tramway from Morda Colliery which had fallen out of use by the end of the 1860s.

Maesbury Hire Cruisers (01691 679963), a sister company of Maesbury Marine Services, offers day and short-term hire craft from the small wharf alongside the winding hole here.

Beyond the bridge the canal is sadly waterless, the preserve of walkers.

Curling round the fields it reaches the B4396 road at Redwith Bridge which, it is hoped, will be accessible by boat in 2006. A new bridge already awaits its first boat.

Gronwen to Pant

Away from the mills the canal continues its remote way through the farmland to Crickheath Wharf, which now sees little disturbance. To judge from the length of the wharf frontage, small stable and the number of cottages gathered around, this must once have been the scene of much clamour and activity. Much of this was generated by the bringing of stone to the canal by tramway from the north west – remains of the embankment descending to the wharf may still be seen, although the traffic passed to the Cambrian Railways line for on-carriage from about 1913

Pant

The dry canal bed continues through to Pant, passing the site of Bridge 86 where a completely new structure is needed.

At Pant another tramway brought limestone down to extensive canal wharves. When the Cambrian Railways line was built, a station was provided here (some of the buildings survive). A complex of bridges were needed over the tramway, which cut right across the station site. Another interesting bridge – Bridge (88) – carries a minor road over the canal and still retains a second arch through which the horsedrawn tramway passed to connect the two wharves on the offside of the canal. A walk up any of the lanes from this bridge will lead to the A483 main road where there is a Post Office and grocery shop (which also provides useful local

MAP 16
Maesbury to Bridge 91

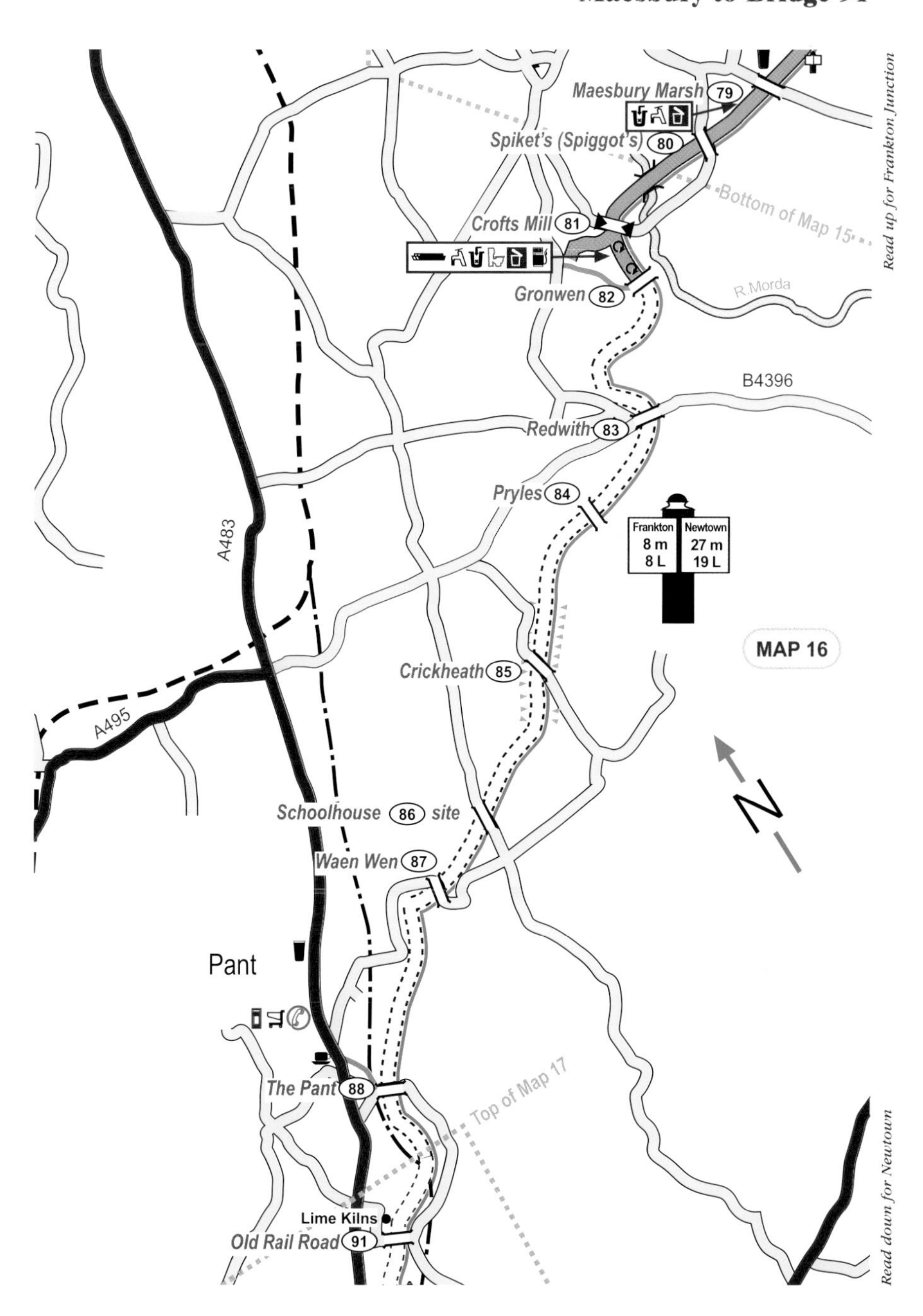

information), a phone box, café and pub. This is the *Cross Guns* (01691 830821) which has Marston's and Banks's beers and food every lunchtime and evening.

Plans for a by-pass to carry A483 traffic around Pant have been threatening the canal here for many years and as a result much of this section is untouched by restoration work. Even the towpath is more neglected than elsewhere and the mileposts are missing.

Bridges 88–93

South of Pant Bridge (88) the condition of the canal is worse than upstream – it is largely filled in. It is possible to walk along the bed or towpath, although several fences add to the exercise involved. Immediately north of Old Rail Road Bridge (91) a further tramway once served a well-preserved bank of five limekilns which dominates the offside bank. A concrete dam under Old Rail Road Bridge serves to separate the infilled canal from the waterless length southwards!

Llanymynech

The Llanymynech Heritage Area is centred on two V-shaped wharf arms of the canal, each of which was served by its own narrow-gauge tramway. The chimney towering out of the trees is a further reminder of the lime-burning industry; it served a Warren continuous lime kiln which is said to have been closed about the time of the First World War because of smoke pollution in the village. Just south of the site of the bridge that carried the railway siding to the kilns over the canal, is the dam that holds back the water, which has entered from the Tanat feeder above carreghofa Locks.

Llanymynech Rocks Nature Reserve incorporates part of the abandoned quarries. Passing under Llanymynech Bridge (92) also entails passing from England into Wales or vice versa.

Llanymynech provides some useful services. There is a selection of pubs; Chinese takeaway and the *Bengal Spices* Indian restaurant (01691 830170), which also offers takeaways; a motor repairer and Post Office, grocer and general store, all handy for the canal bridge. The *Bradford Arms* (01691 830582) offers food every day and has accommodation. The *Cross Keys* (01691 831585) is a Free House with Tetley's and Ansells beers and restaurant and bar food every lunchtime and evening as well as B&B accomodation. Down by the church, *The Lion* is a Bass house. St Agatha's Church is a generally Norman style building but dates only from the 19th century; it has an impressively large clock face.

Walls Bridge (93) to Carreghofa

The far more attractive sight of a watered canal is marred by the fact that the road that should cross Walls Bridge, just south of Llanymynech, contrives to dodge round the structure and cross the canal on the level.

Two small arms extend from the offside of the canal north of Bridge 94 showing where the channel was diverted in 1884 to facilitate construction of the West Shropshire Mineral Railway line, the track bed of which passes under an interesting wrought iron aqueduct beneath the canal here.

Carreghofa Locks

This is a peaceful spot with pleasant canalside cottages and much of interest for the historian or industrial archaeologist. These locks will require to be worked with care making sure to fill the bottom one before emptying the top chamber, as the pound between them is so short that water will be wasted otherwise.

Approaching the top lock, the 'new' feeder from the river Tanat can be seen entering on the offside. Upstream from this feeder is the notional junction between the Ellesmere Canal and the Montgomeryshire Canal. Originally independent of its neighbour, the Montgomeryshire guarded its water supplies carefully (like all canal

Bridge 91 to Maerdy

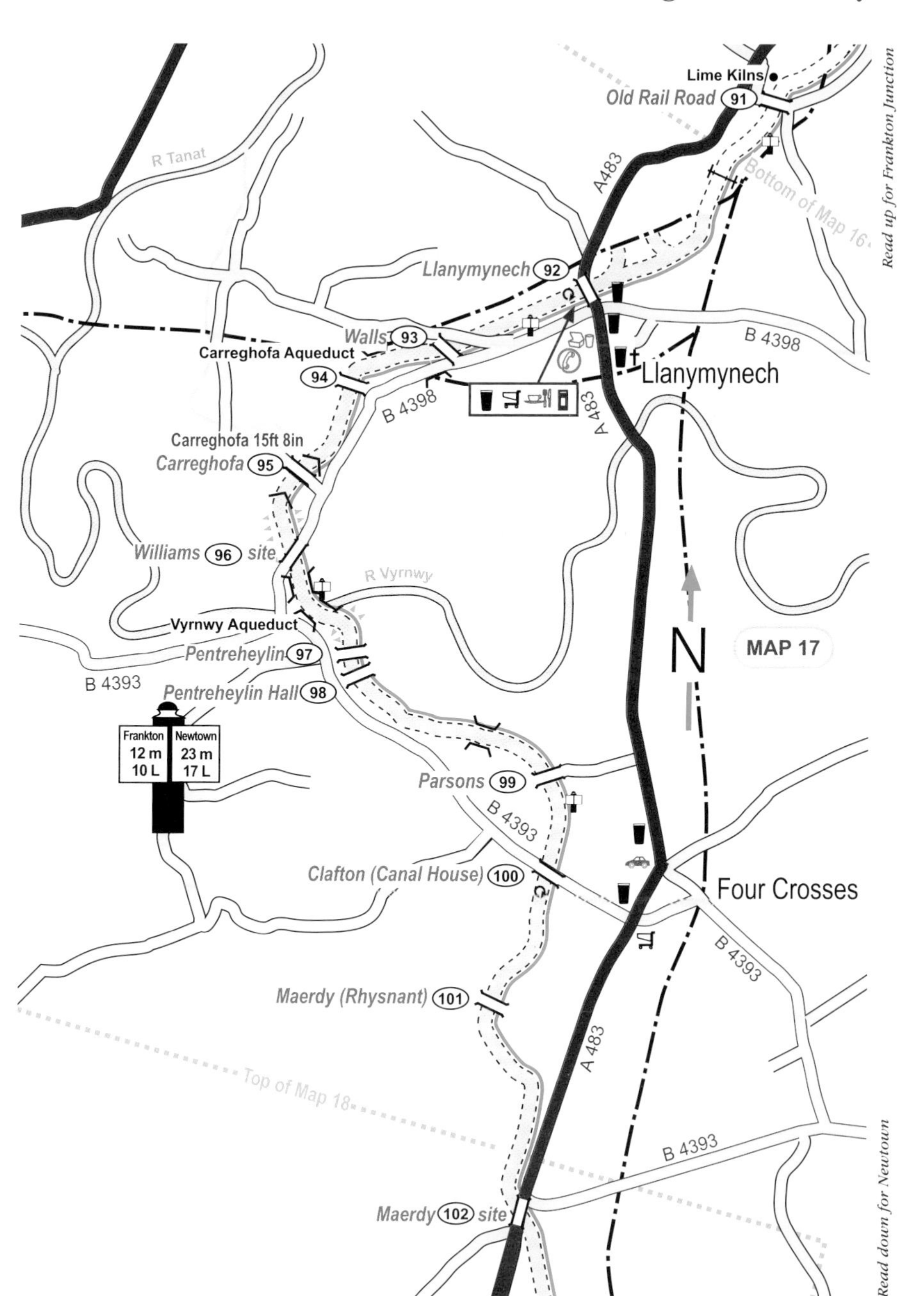

Fred Heritage steers his immaculate ex-Fellows Morton & Clayton motor boat *Lynx* through the new lift bridge at Maesbury Mill during the opening celebrations on this section of canal. At the time it was one of the first ever motorized working boats to use the Montgomery Canal.

companies) and directed its feeder into the pound between the locks so that no drop could inadvertently escape to the benefit of the Ellesmere. Once combined under the Shropshire Union banner these canals shared water and the feeder was diverted to its present course. The old route may be glimpsed from the lane to the west.

The Shropshire Union Canal Society has restored these two locks, and also excavated a 70ft-long flood relief culvert from the restored river Tanat feeder. Two society members are commemorated with a well-placed seat at the top, and the completion of work on a plaque on the toll office across the chamber. Interesting old signs enjoin modern users, as they did those long gone, not to trespass or otherwise misbehave. The complex weir on the offside of the pound controls water levels as it did when the feeder entered there. The lockhouse has a commanding view of boats approaching across the embankment from the Vyrnwy Aqueduct.

Below Carreghofa Locks the canal has been dredged and piled on both sides of the restored Vyrnwy Aqueduct. Much of this work has been completed by BW in order to meet its obligation to feed water to the restored Prince of Wales 'Seven Miles'.

Carreghofa to the Vyrnwy

The canal now strikes out boldly onto an embankment across the river Vyrnwy flood plain over apparently pointless aqueducts built to ensure that the embankment did not obstruct the river's often fierce floods.

This potential drama is soon marred by the sight of William's Bridge (96) one of the most crass and wasteful contributions to canal restoration any local authority has ever made. It was lowered in 1980 when work to restore the two Carrreghofa Locks was already underway, as was work on the Vyrnwy Aqueduct beyond. HRH The Prince of Wales had already given his blessing to the restoration of the canal throughout and reopened a section in Welshpool. This act of municipal vandalism is all the more amazing when you realise that the bridge carried the original main road from Welshpool to Oswestry – but that route had been superceded by the road between Four Crosses and Welshpool now known as the A453 . . . in the 1820s. The outcry was deafening!

The canal crosses the river Vyrnwy on a seemingly substantial aqueduct. The view from the adjacent road bridge, however, tells another the story, with the structure's sag and iron strengthening from major repairs of the 1820s clearly visible. Futher works were needed in the 1890s and 1970s but leaks are still visible.

Vyrnwy Aqueduct to Four Crosses

The waterway swings southeastwards to pass an attractively converted salt warehouse, complete with pillar crane, before following the contours above the river valley towards Four Crosses. There is another small wharf at Clafton (Canal House) Bridge (100), unusually on the towpath side; it is handy for the village but must have been less so for passing horse-drawn boats, which would have to pass their towing lines over moored boats.

No doubt the competing Spar and Cost Cutter shops would have been as welcome to the boatmen as the *Four Crosses Inn* undoubtedly was. The inn has Burtonwood, Boddingtons and Castle Eden ales and offers food every lunchtime and evening – booking for Sunday lunches is a sensible precaution (01691 830184). The Cost Cutter is at the petrol station and sells bottled gas and has a cash machine. Further north along the road is the *Golden Lion,* which has accomodation and offers Banks's and Worthington beers in addition to changing guest ales as well as food.

Bridge 100 to Arddleen

The former turnpike road, now the A483, which has had such a profound effect on the canal since 1944, closes in south of Four Crosses.

At both Maerdy Bridge (102) and Arddleen Bridge (103) the road has been lowered to almost water level and straightened out. However, all is not as

Tranquility in the short pound between the isolated but restored Carreghofa Locks.

John Draddy

bad as it seems. The canal will be dropped by building a new lock above Maerdy Bridge to take the canal below the A483 and Burgedin Top Lock will be reconstructed to reduce its fall. This will have the added benefit of reducing embankments on this length, some stretches of which cause concern in the long term.

Arddleen to Burgedin Locks

Things seem to be looking up when southbound explorers reach Arddleen since the canal is navigable from here southwards to Refail Bridge (129) 11½ miles away. Those northbound and in need of consolation can drown their sorrows at the *Horseshoe Inn* close to the dropped bridge in Arddleen. Bar and restaurant meals are home cooked using fresh produce to go with the selection of real ales which included the products of *Waterways World*'s "local" – Burton Bridge Brewery – on the occasion of our visit! There is also accomodation but the pub is closed Wednesday lunchtime.

Guilsfield Arm

The Guilsfield Arm headed away westwards from the head of Burgedin Top Lock towards the eponymous village, although terminating at a substantial wharf and warehouses just short of the village centre. Now the water is culverted under the B4392 by the locks and the arm beyond preserved as a nature reserve and choked with pond weed. Further along there is little to see but a succession of bridges over a dry ditch.

Burgedin Locks

The Shropshire Union Canal Society has restored the two Burgedin Locks, rebuilt and relined the pound between the locks and had the length immediately above the locks dredged. The cottage at the top lock has been converted into British Waterways Wales Office – possibly the organisation's only office with a fully restored pigsty, even if the latter was being used to dump spare paddle gear on the occasion of our visit. A plaque on the bridge records the reopening of the locks in June 1998 by David Fletcher, then BW Chief Executive. The adjacent roofless and neglected stable is also of interest – being hardly big enough for serious horses. Maybe it was intended only for donkeys. Whatever its purpose, it's original interior fittings will soon be lost if BW does not replace the roof.

Burgedin Locks to The Wern

Below Burgedin Locks is the Montgomery's bottom level – this being an upside down canal that falls from each end to a low mid-point in the Severn Valley. Here is the slipway at The Wern and the beginning of the Prince of Wales' 'Seven Miles' (in fact only 5¾ miles in length) opened by His Royal Highness in 1980 during Prince Charles' third visit to this canal in which he has taken such an interest.

The Wern Red Bridge (106) to Bank Lock

The Wern is a peaceful spot with reminders both of the canal's industrial past and its future in an age of nature conservation and increased leisure time.

Above the bridge is a wharf and winding hole where boats have loaded maintenance materials in recent times. The slipway is a particularly steep one. Don't forget that you will need a BW licence no matter how short your cruise from here; details are on page 4.

Because the locks to both north and south bring boats downhill into this short pound there was always a surplus of water and some of this was put to use at Wern Red Bridge. Just south of the bridge on the towpath side is a large and complex weir. This allowed surplus canal water to drive the waterwheel of the corn mill, whose foundations are close by, whilst at the same time discharging excess water in wet weather to safeguard the canal's banks. The water passed from the mill to

MAP 18
Maerdy to Bridge 109 (Bank Lock)

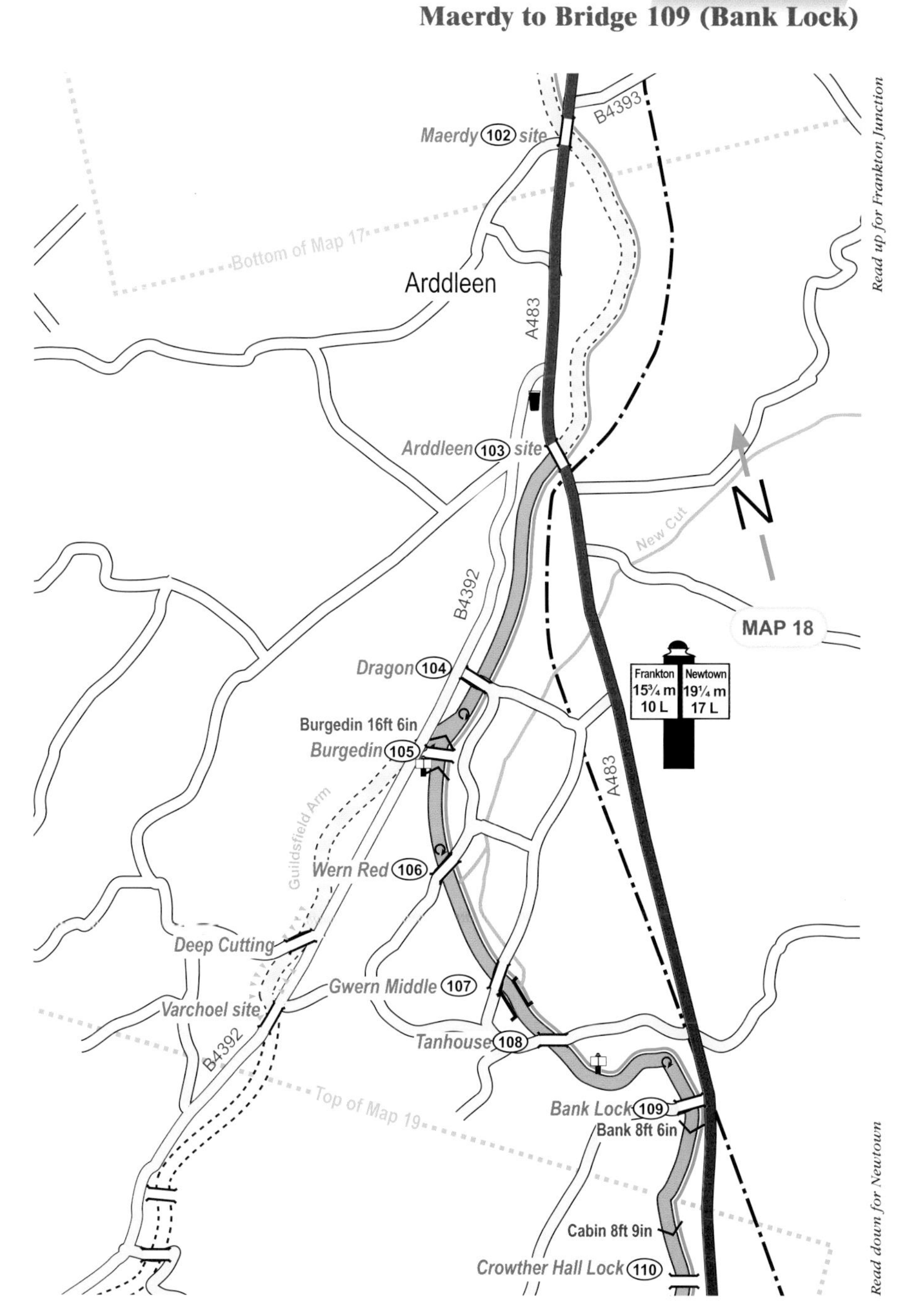

brickworks and so to the 'New Cut' which carries it to the river Severn. Nowadays, the weir discharge twists and turns its way through a nature reserve designed to ensure the survival of plant and animal life that might be disturbed by boat traffic in the canal.

Bank Lock To Pool Quay

The four locks starting the climb towards Newtown (Bank, Cabin, Crowther Hall and Pool Quay) are all restored, following work completed by the Shropshire Union Canal Society and BW. The Briedden Hills command the scene from the east.

Pool Quay was once an important community threaded by the turnpike road and canal, overlooked by the church withits unusual timber belfry. The settlement had grown up at the head of navigation for barges (known as trows, which rhymes with crows) on the river Severn. With the coming of the canal, transhipment of a variety of goods took place between the navigations for which the small warehouses above Pool Quay Lock and, now almost invisible, wharves by the river, were provided. With the improvement of the Severn and construction of locks and weirs below Stourport, trows ceased to be able to venture so far up river and transhipment facilities fell out of use in the mid nineteenth century. By 1904, even the railway station (near Bank Lock and now trackless) was listed as catering only for passengers, parcels, horses and cattle as opposed to the heavier goods of times past. The *Powis Arms* (Worthington) near the main road remains in use however!

Pool Quay Lock signals a pause in the climb towards Newtown for southbound travellers whose numbers, on the towpath at any rate, are increased along this section. The newcomers may well be following the Offa's Dyke Path or the Severn Way which, together, come up from the river and join the towpath at the lock.

Offa's Dyke was provided by Offa (King of Mercia from 757 to 796), but it is not clear if he was intending the considerable earthworks to defend his kingdom or simply mark its boundary. The dyke extends along the Welsh Marches and much of its route is followed by the path from Prestatyn to Chepstow. At Pool Quay the path makes use of the canal towpath although the actual dyke is on the further, eastern, bank of the river Severn. The Offa's Dyke Path only follows the canal for a short distance. Full details of this 182-mile route are available from the Offa's Dyke Centre, West Street, Knighton, Powys LD7 1EN (01547 528753, www.offasdyke.demon.co.uk).

Also joining the towpath at Pool Quay and sharing the route of the Offa's Dyke path at this point, the **Severn Way** keeps company right through to Newtown. Other parts of the route have, as the name would suggest, much of interest to offer waterway enthusiasts since it keeps close company with Britiain's longest river. The path can be followed from the river's source in Hafren Forest on the slopes of Plynlimon for 210 miles to Bristol. For details readers are recommended to the excellent *Severn Way Official Walkers' Guide* by Terry Marsh and Julie Meech (see page 12).

Pool Quay to Buttington

There are moorings and a water tap at Buttington Wharf Bridge (115) where the remains of limekilns survive amongst the trees by a small car park. Buttington village is a short walk away over a fine bridge across the Severn but has little to offer visitors aside from the *Green Dragon* (which does food).

MAP 19
Crowther Hall Lock to Buttington Wharf

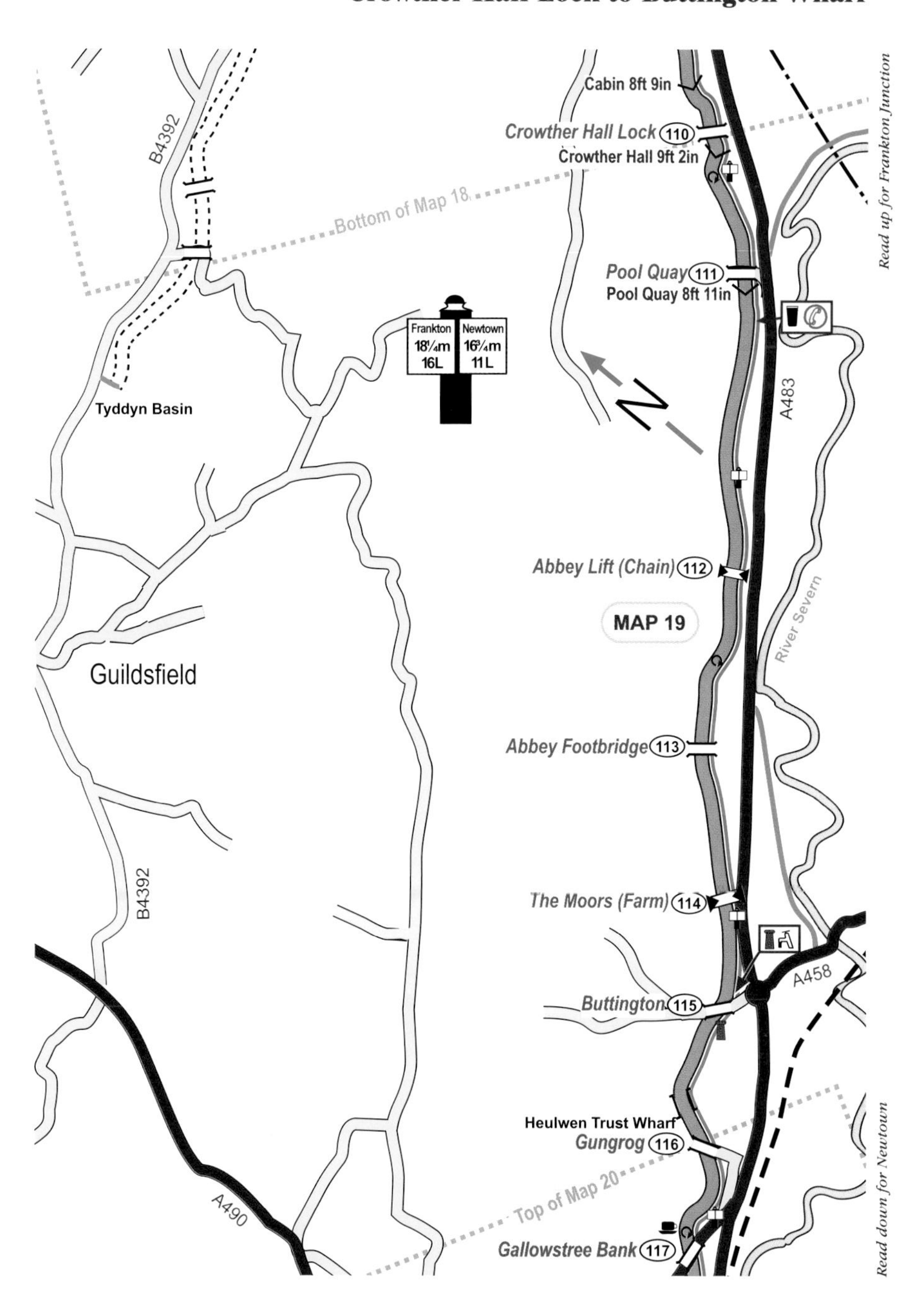

Buttington to Gallowstree Bank Bridge (117)

On Prince Charles' visit to this canal, in 1976, he inaugurated the trip boat for handicapped children *Heulwen–Sunshine*, built by apprentices from Cammell Laird with funds raised by the Variety Club of Great Britain and the ladies of the IWA. The Huelwen Trust (01930 552563) is now based at purpose-built moorings below bridge 116 and operates a day boat and a skippered boat for use by those with disabilities that would otherwise prevent them enjoying the canal.

Gallowstree Bank Bridge (117) to Welshpool

Restoration work on the canal, which started in 1969, was prompted by exceptionally crass proposals to turn the line of the canal beyond Gallowstree Bank Bridge, into a bypass through Welshpool. Apart from the fact that the bypass would have run through the town rather than by-passing it, it is difficult to see how anyone could imagine that the narrow corridor of green tranquility now provided by the canal might be made wide enough to accommodate the breadth of the present dual carriageway bypass road.

The 'Seven Miles' and the navigable two miles through Welshpool, formerly separated by the lowered Gallowstree Bank Bridge, were re-united in 1992 when the bridge was reconstructed with navigable headroom (and a sharp bend on the approach). A small section of the original canal survives as a short arm alongside which walkers must follow the towpath to wander up and down the road in order to make use of the offset zebra crossing. Overlooking the new bridge is the Flash Leisure Centre with a café/restaurant and bar as well as swimming pool, squash and badminton courts, in addition to a wide variety of other opportunities for healthy exercise with all the necessary equipment, sauna steam room and specialist help in the treatment room.

Powysland Tweed Mills, where flannel was once made, were built in the 1830s on the off-side in this section and, by the towpath, a stone wall marks the site of Welshpool's first gas works. These later moved to rail-connected premises. The approach to Clerk's Bridge (118) was lined by several wharves and boatyards, which are now occupied by flats.

Welshpool *All Services, Tourist Information off Church Street*

Beyond Clerks Bridge (118) are moorings and facilities for boats alongside Church Street Car Park which are handy for the town's shops and services. The Tourist Office and a Spar are right by the car park entrance onto Church Street, so there is no real need to explore if you wish to avoid all that this bustling town has to offer!

Welshpool is an important centre for the population of a wide surrounding rural area and received its Market Charter in 1263. The Sheep Market is said to the the largest in Europe and the town has all the services necessary to support its status.

Welshpool Station has been moved a few yards by the promoters of the bus shelter school of architecture, but the old Cambrian Railways station building is worth a visit on its own account as well as for the specialist retail outlets and restaurant it contains.

The restored **Welshpool & Llanfair Light Railway** comes into Raven Square, and is open March to October (01938 810441 or www.wllr.org.uk). The 2ft 6in gauge line used to weave through the town and cross the canal on the girder bridge that now carries a footpath alongside the aqueduct, on its way to the main line station. Originally an important freight carrier, the narrow gauge railway passed from control of the Cambrian Railways through the hands of the Great Western (ceasing to carry passengers in 1931) to become part of British Railways, before closure in 1956. It has been in the care of the preservationists since 1960 and now carries passengers in trains

MAP 20

Bridge 116 (Gungrog) to Bridge 123 (Chapel)

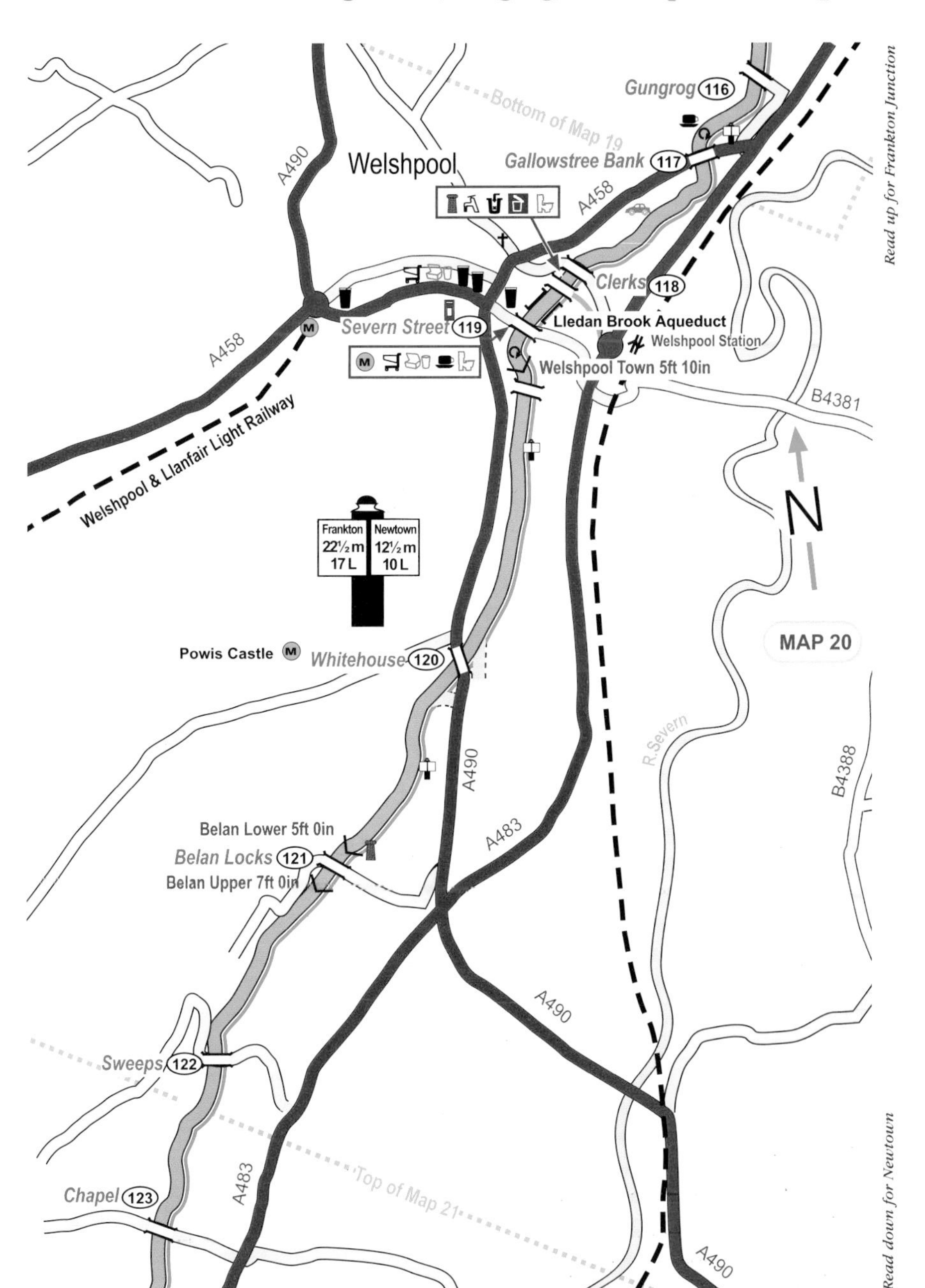

imported from all over the world. The walk to Raven Square Station at the edge of Welshpool is well rewarded by a return trip to Llanfair Caereinion, which takes 50 minutes each way.

The iron aqueduct over the Lledan Brook was built in 1836 with stone arches to carry the towpath. The circular weir was required to feed water to Dommens Mill – one of many such supplies safeguarded by the terms of the canal's enabling Act. The wharf between the aqueduct and Severn Street Bridge (119) was served by a tramway from the Earl of Powis' Standard Quarry (across the roundabout from the present narrow gauge railway terminus) the course of which was later used by the railway.

Welshpool Wharf, formerly used as a highways depot, has been restored by Powys County Council using job creation labour. The former canal warehouse has been converted to house **Powysland Museum** (01938 554656, www.powysmuseums.powys.gov.uk) with displays of local and canal interest. Restored former canal company cottages alongside provide a pleasant backdrop.

Eating places include *Spice:UK* (01938 553431) an Indian restaurant and takeaway on Berriew Street with a seemingly inexhaustible menu which finishes with a note that if you can't find what you want you should ask because "if it's possible we'll be happy to prepare it for you"! One of Wales' top ten fish & chip shops is *Andrews Fish Bar* on High Street, nearby is the Buttery Tea Rooms (01938 552658) and also on High Street is the *Fortune Court* Cantonese restaurant and takeaway (01938 558899) as well as an Indian takeaway. At The Cross on Severn Street is the *Royal Oak Hotel* (01938 552217, www.bestwestern.co.uk) a former coaching inn which offers full hotel services with restaurant meals available every day and Worthington as well as guest real ales in the bars. Near the Market, *The Crown* offers Burtonwood beers and bar meals; it is open all day at weekends.

Indeed, it seems very probable that a walk from Severn Street Bridge, along Broad Street and to the top of the High Street would lead to fulfilment of most peoples' requirements. The *Mermaid* may, or may not, be more politically correct than when it was known as the *Black Boy Inn* but it is an interesting 16th century timber-framed building that has been a pub for 200 years. It is open all day every day. The *Talbot* offers bar meals and games as well as big screen TV. Also on the

The annual 'Dinghy Dawdles' have been a useful source of publicity for the restoration scheme for may years bringing a splash of colour a flurry of activity to the isolated lengths of canal. Here the flotilla locks down at Byles Lock.

High Street and open all day is *The Pheasant* which claims to be 'A traditional Ale House' but shows Sky Sports!

The Market has now largely moved indoors off the street but continues to be held on Mon, Tue, and Saturday in the hall on Broad Street.

One of our reference books points out that cock fighting has been illegal since 1849, which perhaps explains why Welshpools Cockpit on New Street is the only one in Wales still in its original position but not why it has recently been refurbished!

Berriew Street leads from the main traffic lights on Broad Street towards a Somerfield supermarket and a Safeway near Town Lock, via more takeaways and *The Angel*. This street is also worth walking for a fruiterer's and Langford's Food hall with its choice of meats, fish and pies. On the way, notice, if not visit, the Pola Cinema – a well preserved example of 1930s architecture, which now houses two screens, and a night club as well as offering tea, coffee and home cooked meals including breakfast.

Turning the opposite way at the lights, along Church Street, will reveal a National Milk Bar as well as St Mary's Church. Further along, Church Street becomes Salop Road and the *Westwood Park*, which is handy for the moorings, will be reached. It is a Pubmaster house with TV, live music and bar meals.

Welshpool Town Lock

The Prince of Wales has taken a keen interest in the restoration of 'his' seven miles of the canal and on his first visit in 1974 he opened Welshpool Town Lock after its restoration by the Shropshire Union Canal Society. The original, curved, cast iron gates from this lock were removed in 1964 to the Canal Museum at Stoke Bruerne in Northamptonshire.

The excess canal water flowing over the by-wash here was once used to drive a corn mill. Remains of the mounting for the water wheel's shaft in the lockside wall are visible from the car park.

Welshpool to Whitehouse Bridge (120)

Above Town Lock, the car park on the offside incorporates a wharf where coal from Cannock and Wigan was once traded. Opposite is the former Shropshire Union Railways & Canal Co yard which was served by a hand-operated tramway to convey materials and finished products to and from the towpath edge. Notice the surviving rails at the very edge of the path.

The Welshpool to Refail Bridge, Berriew length has undergone substantial work in the more recent past, including international working parties at Belan Locks. Powys County Council started a major project during 1995 to bring this whole length up to navigable standards. The canal line was altered and a new Whitehouse Bridge (120) built (partly funded by the Shropshire Union Canal Society) and usable during 1995. Previously, the A483 crossed the canal on the level, but since construction of the Welshpool bypass, this road (now the A490) has been raised and the canal re-aligned to give navigable headroom and another small nature reserve. Boats should approach slowly and take care around the sharp new bend and past the projecting towpath.

Powis Castle (01938 551929, www.nationaltrust.org.uk) is medieval in origin but contains architecture from many later periods, particularly the 16th and 17th centuries. The 18th century formal gardens are very fine, incorporating enormous clipped yews and sheltering many rare plants. There are lead statues as well as an orangery and aviary. The castle was originally established as a fortress and contains one of Wales' best collections of paintings and furniture. It is home to the Clive family museum, which includes treasures such as textiles, armour, bronzes, jade and ivory brought back from India. The Castle, which is in the care of the National Trust, is open every afternoon from April to October; hours for the gardens, coach house and shop are longer (opening at 11am) but all are closed on Tuesday and Wednesday.

Shortly after passing under Whitehouse Bridge southbound travellers will note the stone wall surrounding Powis Estate Saw Mills at the back of the towpath. The saw mills were once water-powered via a leat from the canal and some interesting remains of the iron trunking and machinery survive. The premises are still in industrial use and so not open to the public except during an annual wood fair in September (details 01938 553785) but gates, flooring and similar substantial timber products are available for purchase at all times. In 2004 applications were being made for listed building consent to restore parts of the buildings and machinery which, if successful, would result in better public access to this historic site.

Belan Locks to Berriew Lock

All four locks needed major work following disuse. Considerable other work was also needed, including a lot of piling.

Brithdir Lock bywash has been enlarged and diverted to create a further nature reserve. Beware of the guard dog at the lock house – if you fish his ball out of the lock chamber he'll throw it over the garden gate and straight back in again, obviously for the pleasure of seeing you fish it out again! You could be there all day but the surrroundings are attractive and there is room to tie up either side of Brithdir Bridge (125) to visit the *Horseshoes* (01686 640282). It serves real ales and bar food every lunchtime and evening with Italian meals a speciality and keeps Banks's and Tetley's beers. In the back garden are limekilns that could once be charged by barrowing limestone and coal directly across the towpath from the boats. Now the canal draws away from the A483 as it enters the Rhiw valley.

A small iron aqueduct preceeds Luggy Bridge (126), which is overlooked by a hillock clothed in magnificent trees that conceal the remains of the local castle.

Berriew Lock to Refail (Efail-Fach) Bridge

Access to Berriew villiage is easy from either the Berriew Long Bridge (128), which was sometimes referred to as the tunnel bridge, or from steps down the side of the aqueduct where there is a picnic place at its southern end.

Near Long Bridge is Silver Scenes (01686 640795, www.silverscenes.com) where silver plated gifts and trophies are made and craftsmen can be seen at work during factory tours daily (Mon–Thur).

Walking under the low span of the aqueduct, which accommodates a lane on the river Rhiw's southern bank, the approach to the village is marred by the ugly, industrial, aspect of the building that houses the Andrew Logan Museum of Sculpture (01686 640689, www.andrewlogan.com) although many will find its contents interesting. It is open Wed–Sun and Bank Holiday afternoons. Beyond the museum it becomes apparent that the village is very picturesque and it is a serial Best Kept Village trophy winner! There is a fine 18th century stone road bridge spanning the rapids in the river Rhiw as it descends to pass under the aqueduct and into the Severn, surrounded by attractive black and white cottages and the church (medieval but rebuilt in Victorian times) set amongst gravestones shaded by mature trees. Of worldly use are the several shops including Post Office, craft shop, butcher and Spar foodstore (which remains open all day every day). If you're exhausted by all this, take a peaceful break in the Woodland Garden near the bridge, a collaboration between the Princes Trust and the Vaynor Estate for the enjoyment of all. Otherwise refreshment may be obtained at the *Talbot* (01686 640881) near the aqueduct where there are Bass and Worthington ales and food is offered in the evenings from Tue to Fri and at lunchtime and evening over the weekend. There is also B&B acomodation. The *Lion Hotel* (01686 640452) fur-

Bridge 123 (Chapel) to Garthmyl

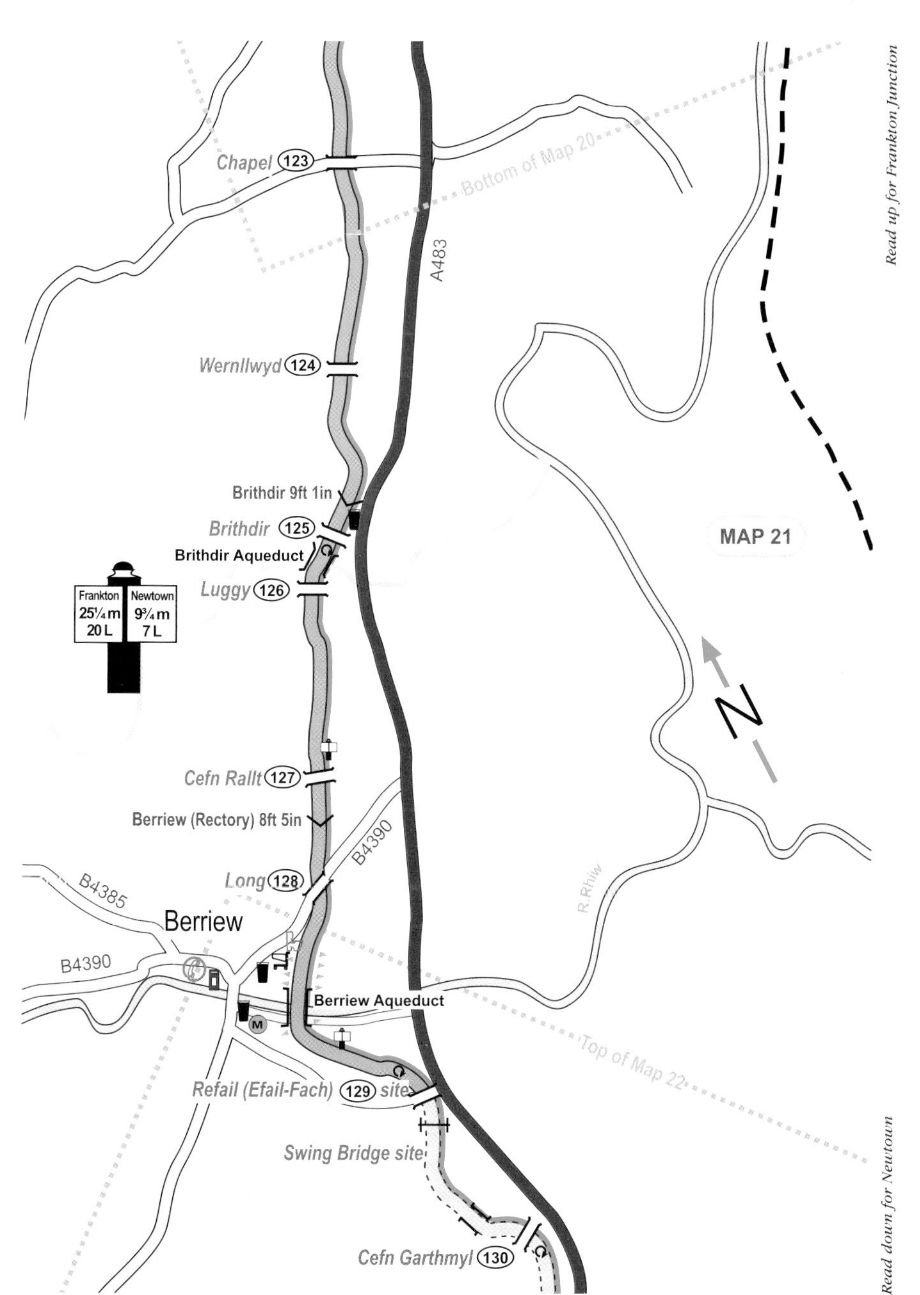

ther through the village also has accommodation and offers home-made restaurant and bar food every lunchtime and evening with the Bass and Worthington joined by changing guest ales.

Berriew Aqueduct over the river Rhiw has repeatedly been a source of anxiety for the canal's engineers; parts collapsed in 1796, major repairs were necessary in 1889, when much of the blue-bricked reconstruction visible to this day was carried out, and a solution was found in 1948 when the water supply was piped over a dried aqueduct. The structure was re-lined and re-watered for navigation in 1984.

The end of the 11½ mile, isolated, navigable section of waterway from Bridge 103 at Arddleen is reached at Refail. There is a wharf and stables by the winding hole here and the B4385 crosses on the site of Refail (Efail-Fach) Bridge (129).

The nearby Spar and newsagents is open every day. Across the main road is the entrance to Glansevern Hall which is open Friday, Saturday and Bank Holiday Monday afternoons in Summer with tea rooms, gallery and shop with plants for sale. There is a handy postbox by the culverted bridge.

Refail (Efail-Fach) Bridge to Garthmyl

Just beyond Cefn Garthmyl Bridge (130) the site of the original terminus of the canal from Welsh Frankton is passed. By the time the canal was opened to Garthmyl in August 1797, money had run out after the trials and tribulations of constructing what became the **Eastern Branch of the Montgomeryshire Canal** from Llanymynech, particularly the Vyrnwy Aqueduct. Three banks of limekilns, maltings, warehouse and stables were established at the terminus along, with the necessary cottages for their workforce.

The **Montgomeryshire Canal's Western Branch** onwards to Newtown was only constructed through the determination and financial support of William Pugh of Brynllywarch, near Kerry, who is said to have put over £50,000 of his own fortune into the works. The canal was complete to Newtown by the end of 1821 but Pugh never recovered his investment and died in France in 1842 deep in debt. George Buck was again the engineer, before moving to work on railway construction under Robert Stephenson.

Garthmyl

Nags Head Bridge (132) was one of the earliest to be dropped after legal abandonment of the navigation under the 1944 Act. The culvert extends from Bridge 131 (which still stands on the original line of the A483) to the far side of the road junction and proudly bears bricks dated 1949.

Facing the main road is the *Nag's Head,* which is closed on Wednesday but serves food lunchtime and evening (except Sunday evening) in restaurant and bar, and Bishops Castle and Worthington beers. There is a garden and accomodation.

Trwstllewelyn Aqueduct (132B) has been rebuilt in concrete together with the adjacent storm weir. This has resulted in the water level being lowed about 8in – it is to be hoped that this pound is to be dredged accordingly to restore the depth before it becomes accessible to larger craft.

Garthmyl to Brynderwyn

From Half Way Bridge (136), which was another of the early culvertings of 1949, the A483 follows close by, its traffic destroying the peace of the canal through otherwise beautiful scenery. There is a succession of small bridges, some fixed swinging spans, immediately alongside the main road.

MAP 22
Garthmyl to Bridge 144 (Bryn Turn)

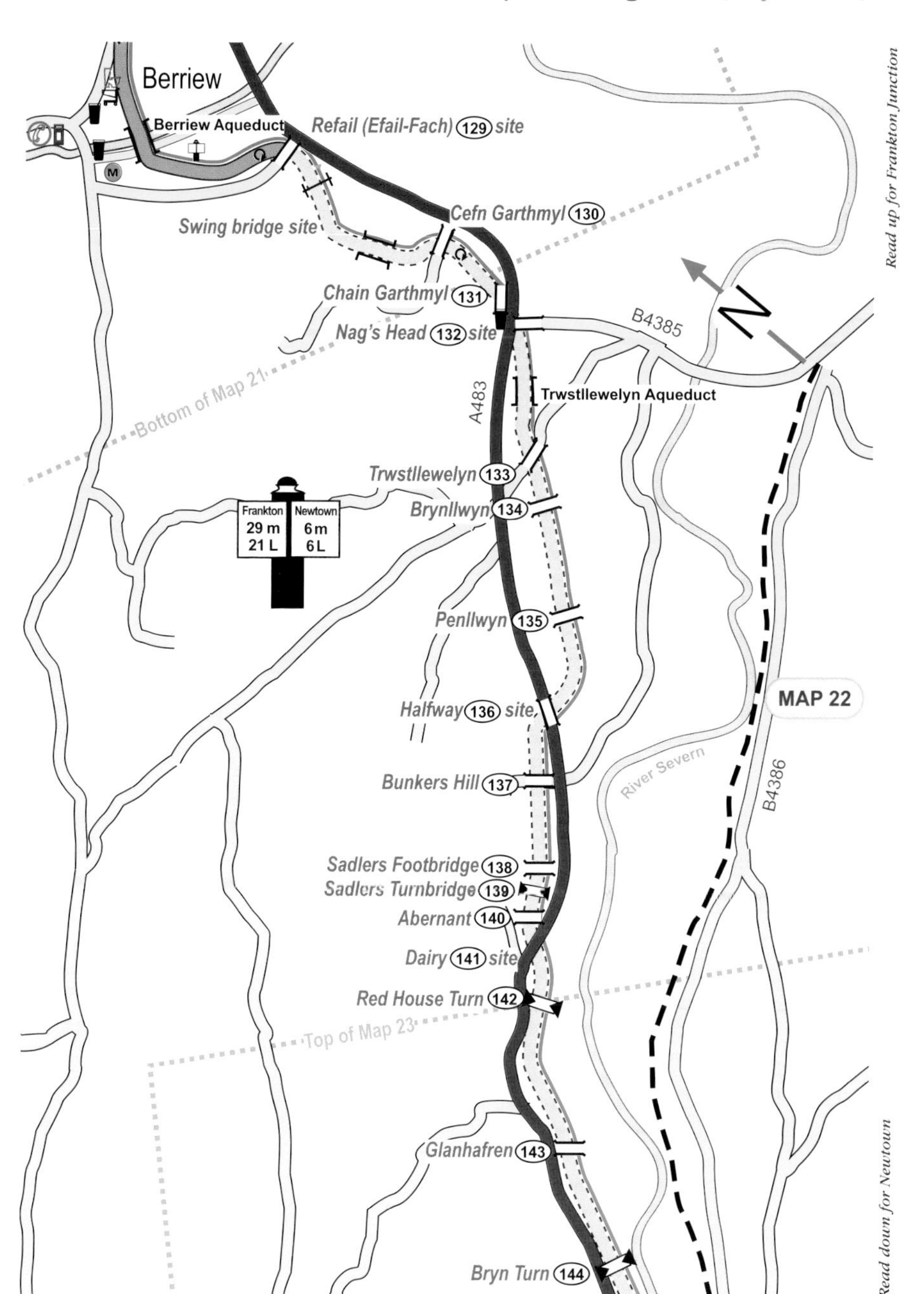

Euan Corrie

At times of low water in the river Rhiew it is possible to see this view of the Montgomery Canal's crossing on Berriew Aqueduct.

Brynderwyn to Freestone Lock

At Brynderwyn Wharf Bridge (145) the towpath changes sides past a wharf so that towing lines would not interfere with the moored boats. By Brynderwyn Lock there is a standard canal company brick and corrugated iron warehouse close against the busy road. Take great care if you wish to view the original Shropshire Union Railways & Canal Company notice which survives on the road elevation; there is little shelter from those drivers who use either side of the road without regard for speed limits here. Smaller plaques on the lock side give details of the Shropshire Union Canal Society's restoration of the warehouse in 1993 and of the reopening of the lock itself in 2002.

Abermule

At Brynderwyn New Road Bridge (147) the road is carried over the canal on iron girders bearing a Brymbo Ironworks plate dated 1853 – but turn aside for a moment for a view of the magnificent statement of local pride on the river bridge's impressive iron arch alongside (dated 1852). The road over these bridges provides the safest, if not the shortest, route into Abermule where there is a useful Post Office and stores with ice cream and provisions.

The *Abermule Hotel* (01686 630676) serves good, substantial, bar meals every lunchtime and evening as well as Tetley real ales and has a camping and caravan site behind. The *Waterloo* opposite the village Post Office has cask ales and bar food. Behind it is a tidy and very well equipped independent caravan site.

Abermule has been a name well-known to any with an interest in railways since midday on 26th January 1921 when an express from Aberystwyth to Manchester collided head on with a local train from Whitchurch a mile south of the, since closed, village station on the single track

Bridge 144 (Bryn Turn) to Brechan Brook Aqueduct

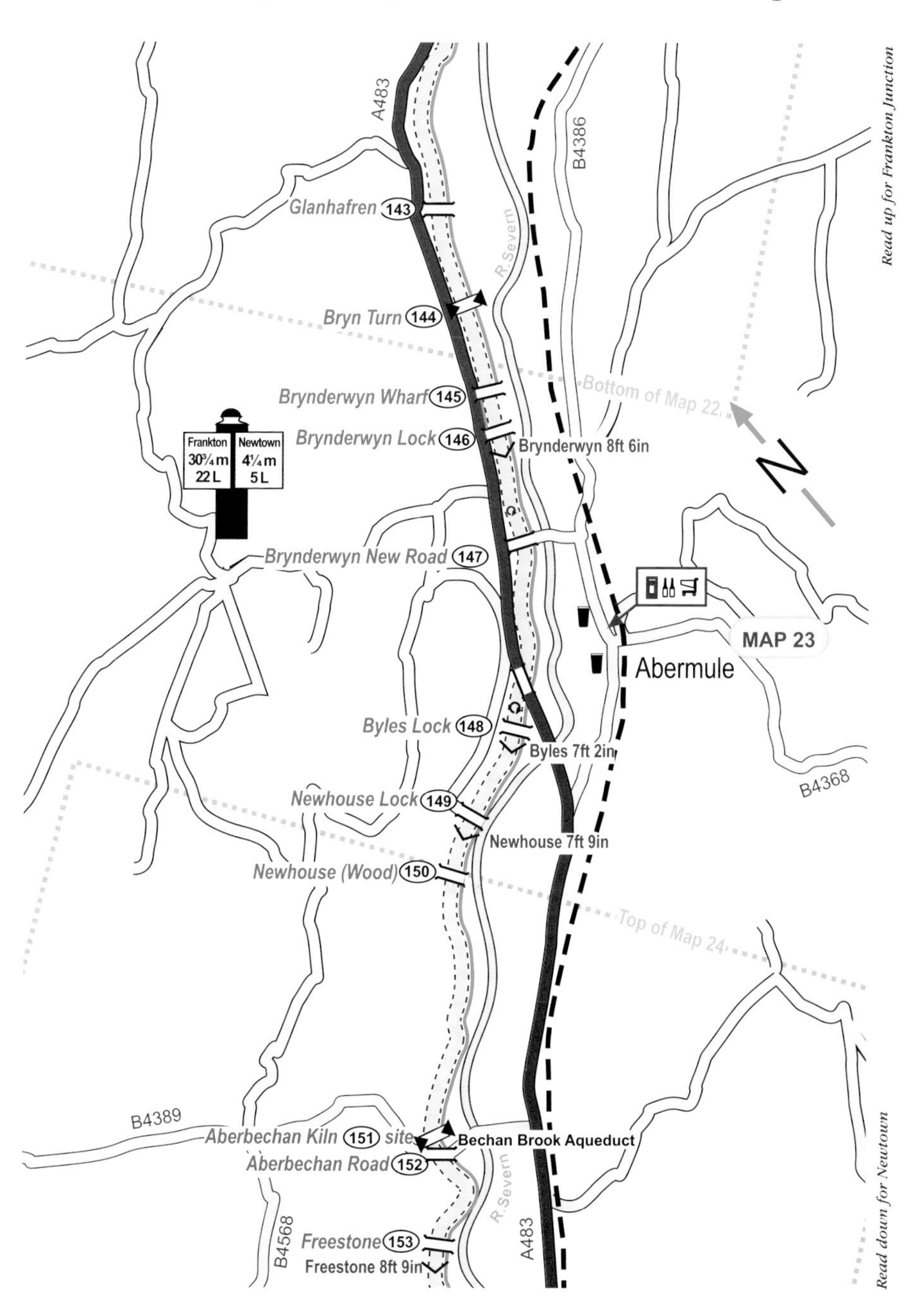

railway which parallels the canal. The collision occurred on a section of the Cambrian Railway that was fully equipped with efficient mechanical and electrical safety devices. However, these were totally defeated by several different members of the staff who broke operating regulations and failed to work together as a team, so despatching the local passenger train into the section of track between Abermule and Newtown – already occupied by the express. Fourteen passengers and three railwaymen were killed.

Amongst the nearby culverted bridges, Abermule Bypass (A483) bridge offers a note of optimism for navigators. However it is more of a navigable culvert than a traditional canal bridge and walkers must follow the Severn Way signs and head towards the river Severn to pass under the road through one of the flood-relief spans alongside the river. Regaining the towpath beyond, the bypass walkers will be pleased to find the road moving away from the canal and peace returning.

The next lock, Byles, was re-gated by BW to enable them to move their dredging equipment up the canal to clear the channel for water coming down from the Penarth feeder.

At Aberbechan Kiln Bridge (151) (a fixed swing bridge) the remains of once busy maltings and a corn mill may be glimpsed in the trees and the canal soon crosses the Bechan Brook on a small aqueduct. Beyond, Aberbechan Road Bridge (152) is another product of Brymbo Ironworks, which seems to have been busy with canal work in 1863.

Freestone Lock to Newtown Terminal Basin

Those walking from Newtown will find that their surroundings improve dramatically as they pass Freestone Lock. The feeder from Penarth Weir on the river Severn enters immediately below the lock and the canal channel northwards contains water. It is possible to walk towards the river, by the Pwll Penarth Nature Reserve, via a footpath from the head of the lock which leads to the point where a paddle controls the flow of water through a culvert into the canal. The open feeder channel may be followed northwards to the weirs on the river Severn. These were built between 1814 and 1818 and incorporate a salmon ladder.

South of Freestone Lock, and on towards Newtown, a footpath follows the line of the canal towpath but although the waterway is largely filled in many traces remain. There are also information boards describing the surrounding historical remains. Studies started in 2003 into the possibilities of incorporating a restored canal into proposed housing developments on the outskirts of Newtown.

Newtown Basin

The superb basin in Newtown itself, well, just across the river from the town, was filled in along with the canal to Freestone. It is difficult to imagine that once there were no less than 22 limekilns on the land between the basin and the river. The basin had several side arms and was at one time lined with warehouses, coal yards, timber and merchandise wharves and, naturally, several inns. Some buildings survive, including cottages, stables and the *Waggon & Horses,* which can offer bar meals.

Newtown *All services, Tourist Information at The Park on Back Lane*

Newtown lays claim to being the largest town in mid-Wales and has expanded dramatically since flood defences were improved after inundation in the 1960s. The Tourist Information Centre can offer free leaflets detailing the town's history and walks that will do much to bring its past alive as well as details of local transport, sustenance and accommodation. One of the town's most famous inhabitants was Robert Owen, an industrialist who did much to further the aims of the Co-operative movement. A museum (01686 626345) recalling his life and work,

MAP 24
Brechan Brook Aqueduct to Newtown

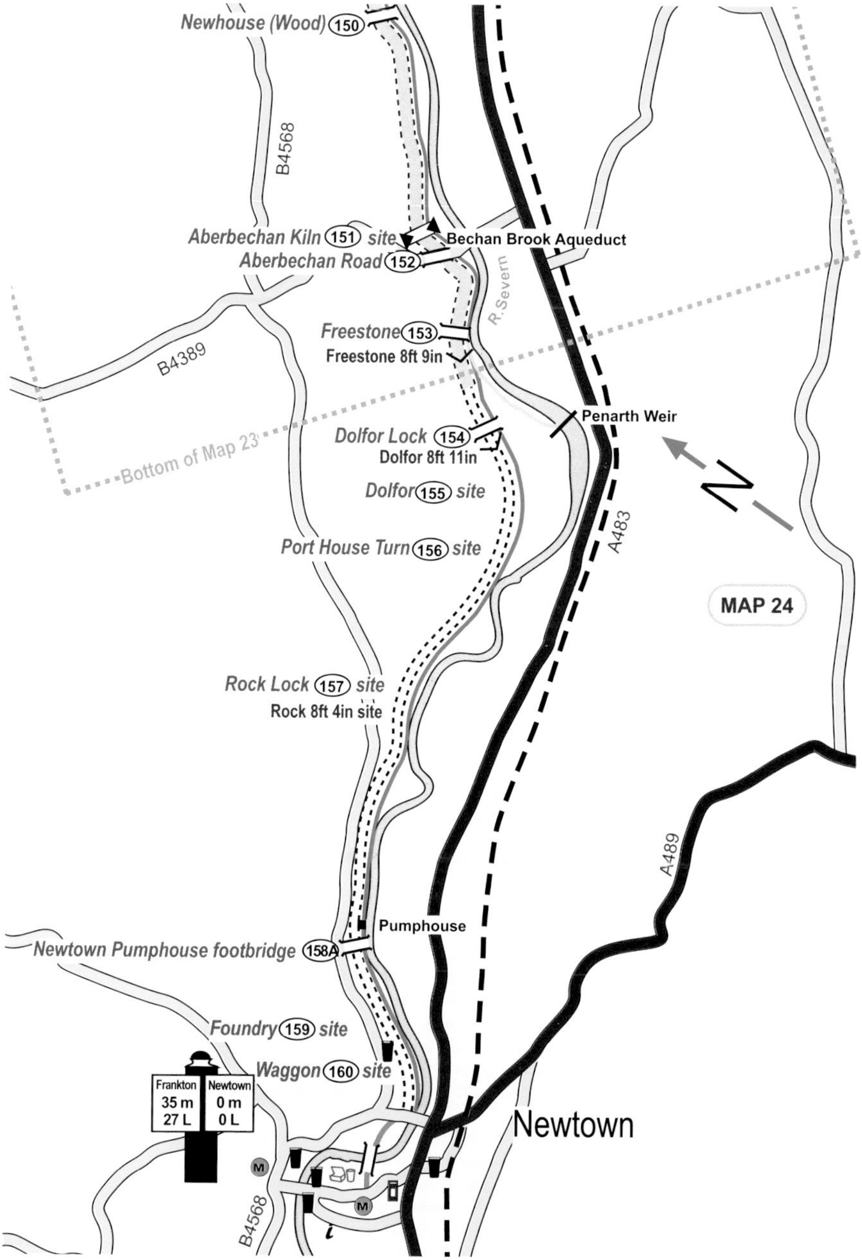

Read up for Frankton Junction

Newhouse (Wood) 150

B4568

Aberbechan Kiln 151 site

Bechan Brook Aqueduct

Aberbechan Road 152

R. Severn

Freestone 153

Freestone 8ft 9in

B4389

Penarth Weir

Dolfor Lock 154

Dolfor 8ft 11in

Bottom of Map 23

Dolfor 155 site

A483

Port House Turn 156 site

MAP 24

Rock Lock 157 site

Rock 8ft 4in site

A489

Pumphouse

Newtown Pumphouse footbridge 158A

Foundry 159 site

Waggon 160 site

Frankton	Newtown
35 m	0 m
27 L	0 L

Newtown

B4568

in New Lanark as well as Newtown, is at the corner of Broad Street and Severn Street and is open weekday mornings and afternoons and Saturday mornings.

Newtown Textile Museum, (01938 554656, www.powysmuseums.powys.gov. uk) is a remarkable survival of six back-to-back cottages on the ground floor with a nineteenth century hand-loom weaving shop on the upper floors where the families resident below worked. It tells the story of their lives from the 1830s to the decline of the woollen industry in the 20th century and of Newtown's industries in general. It is open on Mon, Tue and Thur–Sat afternoons May–Sept.

Euan Corrie

Another of Newtown's claims to fame is that local draper Pryce Pryce-Jones, realising the potential to reach distant markets offered by the railways, set up the world's first mail order business here in 1859. He sent out bolts of local cloth and manufactured garments. However, his striking Royal Welsh Warehouse, near the station, which dates from 1879, was built to cater for cheaper cloth imported from the large mechanised mills of Lancashire and Yorkshire and may be seen as a symbol of the decline of the local industry. It is still used for mail order today.

W. H. Smith's shop at 24 High Street (01686 626280) has been restored to its condition when opened in 1927, providing a fascinating contrast to the company's shops elsewhere. Upstairs is an interesting museum (open 9am to 5.30pm Mon–Sat) telling the company's (and family's) history. Most national chain stores are represented within a short walk of the High Street.

There are plenty of opportunities to re-fuel boat crews unaccustomed to having to walk an unrestored canal, or indeed to re-fuel experienced towpath walkers! The *Bell* (01686 625540) on Commercial Street enjoys *Good Beer Guide* listing for its Greene King and Old Speckled Hen and offers restaurant and bar meals every lunchtime and evening; The *Black Boy* on Broad Street has Tetley's and a salad bar and carvery every lunchtime and evening; up by the bridge is the *Elephant & Castle* also offering real ale and meals, with the addition of Sky TV. Opposite is the Flannel Exchange, built in 1832 by William Pugh to house the market transferred from Welshpool. Its cellar now houses *The Exchange* which also offers bar meals. In the High Street *The Buck* is a Banks's house with bar meals available. If you require Indian food with your Theakstons (or one of the guest ales) head for the *Cross Guns* on Park Street any lunch time or evening; there's also accommodation and a garden. Those seeking an unspoilt local might try the *Railway Tavern* on Old Kerry Road where there is good Bass, Worthington and guest beers to go with darts and dominoes. On Severn Street *The Sportsman* offers Ansells with its bar meals and seems surrounded by takeaways of many persuasions, not to mention the launderette.